Jars of Clay

What the West needs to learn from the persecuted Church

Kenneth Harrod

Foreword by the Archbishop of York

Release International

Through its international network of missions, Release International serves persecuted Christians in thirty countries around the world by supporting pastors and Christian prisoners and their families, supplying Christian literature and Bibles, and working for justice.

Romanian pastor Richard Wurmbrand, who was imprisoned and tortured by the Romanian authorities for a total of 14 years, inspired the founding of Release in 1968.

Richard Wurmbrand died in February 2001, but his vision and passion to serve persecuted Christians around the world continues in the ministry of Release today.

For further information, please contact:

Release International
PO Box 54
ORPINGTON
Kent
BR5 4RT

Tel: 01689 823491   Email: info@releaseinternational.org

or visit our website: www.releaseinternational.org

Jars of Clay

What the West needs to learn from the persecuted Church

We have this treasure in jars of clay, to show that the surpassing power belongs to God and not to us.

(2 Corinthians 4:7)

release INTERNATIONAL
voice of persecuted christians

Cover Design by Claire Pepperd

COMMENDATIONS

Kenneth Harrod has written an extremely timely reminder to the church in the West that the persecution of Christians is not just some unfortunate manifestation of opposition to the faith that crops up from time to time in far-flung places but is absolutely central to Christian discipleship. We may or may not face persecution ourselves but if we fail to understand this aspect of the faith we will be much the poorer for it. New Testament Christians understood the cost of following Jesus and were prepared to pay the price. Harrod's little book will help Christians in the West refocus on the really important, and sometimes costly, aspects of our faith. If you've ever had the feeling that something is missing from your Christian life, read this book and your idea of church and discipleship may never be the same again!

Canon Andrew White
Chaplain of St George's Church, Baghdad.

- - -oOo- - -

For the past 35 years I have had the privilege of working with persecuted Christians from around the world. In that time I have learnt so much from them that has made me a stronger person in my own walk with God. In this excellent little book Kenneth Harrod looks at the lessons we can learn from our worldwide persecuted family which, if applied to our own lives, will make us better and more effective disciples of Jesus.

The theology of persecution sounds like a very heavy topic - and indeed it can be! However, *Jars of Clay* brings out the major themes of the theology of persecution in a very practical way. Indeed Kenneth clearly makes the point that for Christians in the West, engaging with the issue of persecution should not be just about praying and providing for our persecuted family, but that it should also be about walking and learning with them the lessons of discipleship.

It is a subject rarely taught in our churches but I would suggest that leaders should buy this book and use it as a basis for teaching in their churches and small groups. The church in the free West will grow much stronger if it learns the key lessons from our persecuted brothers and sisters that are brought out here by Kenneth Harrod.

Mervyn Thomas
Chief Executive
Christian Solidarity Worldwide

- - -oOo- - -

Iraq, Nigeria, India, Egypt. The rise of persecution against Christians is a significant phenomenon across the world today. Kenneth Harrod's book is timely – and it makes a compelling and biblically-based case for engaging with the parts of the worldwide church which are facing persecution.

In *Jars of Clay* Kenneth skilfully navigates the documents of the New Testament, helping us to picture what persecution meant for the Early Church. From these pages we see that the threat of persecution isn't a matter that can be confined to history or other cultures, but is a challenge to our notion of how the church should be following Jesus today.

I believe every Christian has something to learn from the persecuted church. And that's why this book is important. Because it helps us - in a lucid and accessible way - to be ready. Ready to serve our persecuted brothers and sisters. Ready to serve God as jars of clay. Ready, if necessary, to meet threat or opposition ourselves for following Him.

Brother Andrew says in *God's Smuggler*, "Persecution is an enemy the church has met and mastered many times. Indifference could prove to be a far more dangerous foe."

Either way, may this book help us learn and be prepared.

Lisa Pearce
Chief Executive
Open Doors UK and Ireland

- - -oOo- - -

Release International is thrilled to publish this book. Persecution, and the idea of suffering for the sake of Christ, is absolutely central to New Testament Christianity and Christian discipleship. In fact, most of the New Testament was written when persecution was centre-stage, and from the perspective that sharing in the sufferings of Christ was, and always would be, the norm for Christians. It follows therefore that engaging seriously with the issue of persecution can only help to bring biblical truth to bear on our own lives and on the life of our churches today. I believe that this book by Kenneth Harrod will help you to learn the very same lessons that the early church learned and that countless persecuted believers around the world are learning again today – what it truly means to be a follower of Jesus Christ.

We might not face the threat of violence or mortal danger for our Christian faith but we can all learn with those who do. If our hearts are open to God's leading we can all learn together more of what it means to offer ourselves daily as living sacrifices, holy and pleasing to God. Archbishop Ben Kwashi of Nigeria said, 'If God spares my life no matter how short or long that is, I have something to live for, something worth living and dying for. This world is not our home; we are strangers here, we've got business to do, let's get on and do it.'

As you read this book, either on your own or as part of a study with others, you may never look at your Christian life in the same way again!

Paul Robinson
Chief Executive
Release International

Dedication

To the staff of Release International, and
to the glory of God.

Contents

Contents

Foreword

In the so-called liberal democracies of the West today we are surprised and shocked when we hear of discrimination and violence against believers in other less 'tolerant' parts of the world. And yet too often we lack the magnanimity to embrace, as we should, the struggles of those who are at the (literally) sharp end of today's conflicts. This book will help us attend to their cry, and learn from the grace of their sufferings in Christ. Misunderstandings and hostilities of a religious kind, when allied with social, economic, tribal, and ethnic divisions, are the cause of much suffering and loss of life today. And yet this is nothing new.

From earliest times the followers of Jesus have faced opposition and persecution. I like to recall this text from the second century *Epistle to Diognetus*, possibly written as early as 124 AD, which gives a characteristic picture of Christian people at the time:

They dwell in their own countries, but simply as sojourners. As citizens, they share in all things with others, and yet endure all things as if foreigners. Every foreign land is to them as their native country, and every land of their birth as a land of strangers.......They are in the flesh, but they do not live after the flesh. They pass their days on earth, but they are citizens of heaven. They obey the prescribed laws, and at the same time surpass the laws by their lives. They love all men, and are persecuted by all. They are unknown and condemned; they are put to death, and restored to life. They are poor, yet make many rich; they are in lack of all things, and yet abound in all; they are dishonoured, and yet in their very dishonour are glorified. They are evil spoken of, and yet are justified; they are reviled, and bless; they are insulted, and repay the insult with honour; they do good, yet are punished as evil-doers. When punished, they rejoice as if quickened into life; they are assailed by the Jews as foreigners, and are persecuted by the Greeks; yet those who hate them are unable to assign any reason for their hatred.

To speak in general terms we may say that the Christian is to the world what the soul is to the body. As the soul is present in every part of the body, while remaining distinct from it, so Christians are found in all cities of the world, but cannot be identified with the world. It is by the soul, enclosed within the body, that the body is held together, and similarly it is by these Christians, detained in the world as in a prison, that the world is held together.'

(Extract from *Epistle to Diognetus*, Ch 5-6)

In all our vision and planning for mission today, we should hold on to the glory of Christ, and heed the voice of the weak, of those persecuted for their faith in Jesus Christ, in whom God's power and the authority of Christ is revealed. For me, a guiding light in my life has always been the memory of the radiant faith of the Martyr Janani Luwum, Archbishop of Uganda, Rwanda, Burundi and Boga Zaire, and his Christ-like compassion, simplicity, humility, and joy, even as he faced the certainty of his suffering and death. His last words to his brother bishops as he was led away the last time were, 'Do not be afraid. I see God's hand in this.'

In the face of consumerist religion, the call to new life in Christ and to follow him in company with others, and to suffer with him, may not be popular. But to be true to our roots, we must heed this call – we neglect it at our peril, and, as St Paul rightly says to us, *'God's foolishness is wiser than human wisdom, and God's weakness is stronger than human strength.'* 1 Corinthians 1:25. The fruit of such faithfulness is glory to God, made manifest in all those who take up their cross, and follow Christ for the sake of the world for which Christ died and rose again. They would rather suffer wrong than do wrong, as the greatest conquest of all hatred is to turn enemies into friends.

May God give us all grace to follow his saints in the footsteps of Jesus Christ and his suffering saints – in faith, and hope and love.

+Sentamu Eboracensis   Holy Week 2015

Introduction

"Life is the art of avoiding pain."

*Thomas Jefferson, US President, 1801-1809,
writing in 1786*

"We rejoice in our sufferings."

*The Apostle Paul, writing to Christians in
Rome, first century*

Which of those two sentiments do you find it easier to identify with?

If we're honest, I suspect many of us would probably choose the former. After all, suffering is not something we ever contemplate with relish.

Those of us who live in the West have grown up in a world where comfort and ease are assumed to be among our basic rights. Pain and suffering are not part of the deal, and are meant to be avoided at all costs. Even many of us who profess to be followers of Jesus Christ have perhaps bought into this mindset without realising it, or

1

thinking much about it. Being a Christian, after all, is surely all about *joy*, isn't it?

Well, yes, in so many respects that may be true. The Christian life should be characterised by the joy that knowing Jesus Christ brings. But that is not the whole picture, this side of eternity.

This is a book about suffering: in fact, about a particular form of suffering. Not the suffering that is common to all mankind: the suffering that might be caused by illness, bereavement, natural disasters or the apparently random ups and downs of human existence – significant though all of those things are. No, this is a book about the kind of suffering that comes our way *because* we are followers of Jesus Christ. When others deliberately cause that suffering, we generally refer to it as 'persecution'.

Christians in the West don't, on the whole, think about persecution as much as we should. That's not altogether surprising, as serious persecution has not been a major factor for Christians in our part of the world for many years. Occasionally, we are alarmed by changing attitudes toward Christianity in our own, increasingly secular, society but, for the most part, persecution doesn't loom large in our thinking and praying.

For some, persecution is what happened in the early centuries of the Christian era, before Emperor Constantine legalised Christianity. For others, persecution is something that has occurred at certain pivotal moments in history, such as the Protestant Reformation. Others might say that persecution, regrettably, still happens today in places where, for various historic and cultural reasons, people are oppressed and lack the freedoms we have long enjoyed in the more enlightened West. When we hear of persecution, we are of course appalled. We might even be moved from time to time to pray, "Dear Lord, help and protect those who are persecuted for their faith. Amen."

But persecution, and the idea of suffering for (and even *with*) Christ, is absolutely central to New Testament Christianity and Christian discipleship. In fact, most of the New Testament was written when persecution was centre-stage, and from the perspective that suffering for Christ was, and always would be, the norm for Christians. The Gospels record Jesus telling his disciples, "You will be hated by all for my name's sake" (Matthew 10:22) and, "If they persecuted me, they will also persecute you" (John 15:20). Toward the end of his life, the Apostle Paul comes to the conclusion, "Indeed, all who desire to live a godly life in Christ Jesus will be persecuted" (2 Timothy 3:12). In similar fashion, the Apostle Peter writes, "Beloved, do not be surprised at the fiery trial when it comes upon you to test you, as though something strange were happening to you. But rejoice insofar as you share Christ's sufferings" (1 Peter 4:12,13).

This first-century New Testament perspective can often present problems for Western Christians as we read and study our Bibles. Our first reaction is that this simply isn't our experience – and it hasn't been the experience of the church for several centuries.

Not surprisingly – as more than one writer on the theme of persecution has noted – a consequence of this is that, in our desire to make Scripture relevant to our lives today, we can inadvertently water down passages that are primarily concerned with suffering *for the sake of Christ*.

Take the majestic second half of Romans 8 as an example. The Apostle Paul begins this section of his letter with the bold declaration, "For I consider that the sufferings of this present time are not worth comparing with the glory that is to be revealed to us" (Romans 8:18). This is a wonderful promise and a reminder that, as Christians, we have a sure and certain hope for the future. (We will be considering 'hope' later in this book.) His argument then builds to that glorious conclusion that ultimately nothing "will be able to separate us from the love of God in Christ Jesus our Lord" (Romans 8:39). These are such stirring, encouraging words for every believer to read! It is no wonder that many Christians cite this as one of their favourite passages in the Bible.

But what kind of suffering does Paul have in mind here? Are there any clues? Well, yes, there are. In the previous verses he speaks of the Holy Spirit bearing witness with our spirit that we are children of God and heirs with Christ – and then adds this telling remark (often ignored in sermons and Bible studies): "… provided *we suffer with him* in order that we may also be glorified with him" (Romans 8:17).

In other words, as Paul writes of 'sufferings' in verse 18, it seems he is not thinking of the many and varied sufferings that are the common experience of mankind, but rather is referring primarily to the experience of the Christian who identifies with Christ, who lives and speaks for Christ – and who suffers as a result. This doesn't mean that the great promises of Romans 8 have *nothing* to offer the Christian who is suffering through illness, bereavement or depression. It is, however, an important reminder that, when we are reading and studying God's word, it is always helpful to begin by asking ourselves what the writer is actually saying, and why he is saying it! And when it comes to New Testament references to suffering, that means we would do well to ponder first what it means to be willing to suffer for Christ and his gospel – and what we can learn from this – before applying such references to other, more general forms of suffering in this life.

And 'suffering for Christ' is what this book is all about.

During my work on this project, colleagues periodically referred to the fact that I was writing 'a theology of persecution'. The phrase sounded a little daunting. For some Christians today, the word 'theology' suggests a weighty, academic tome, laden with footnotes referencing other weighty tomes. Worse still, some would identify 'theology' with an intellectual, ivory-tower approach to the things of the Christian faith that has little *practical* relevance for the proverbial 'man or woman in the pew'.

But, in any case, what do we mean by a theology of persecution? What would a theology of persecution include? At least three things, I would suggest. First, it ought to expound the *biblical* reasons why Christians suffer persecution for their faith and witness. There might be all sorts of cultural, ideological and political reasons why Christians face opposition in our complex world, but are there deeper spiritual reasons we can identify?

Secondly, it ought to clarify the counsel Scripture gives about how to respond in the face of persecution: that is, when we experience it ourselves (in whatever form it takes). And thirdly, it ought to set out what pointers

Scripture gives as to how to respond and act when we are aware of *other* Christians suffering for their faith.

All three of these facets are in fact addressed at different points through the course of this book. Nevertheless, none of them constitutes the central purpose of the book.

Mission agencies in the West will encourage you to be aware of persecution in our world today and to respond, by praying, in an informed and specific way, and by giving financially to support work that assists persecuted Christians. And quite right, too. Indeed, we will say more about these matters in the conclusion.

But if persecution - suffering for Christ's sake – is such a central theme in the New Testament, there is more to it than that. As we will explore in this book, we in the West have much to learn from persecution about what it really means to be a Christian, much that would deepen, strengthen and motivate our own faith, individually and collectively.

This is the central purpose of this book. If we are to learn from persecution, it is important that we allow the teaching of the Bible to inform us and to shape our thinking, our understanding of what is happening around the world, and our response to it. Therefore, this book is not, first and foremost, *anecdotal*, even though, for the sake of illustration, I make occasional references to incidents of persecution. There are plenty of places – in books, mission society magazines and, increasingly, on the internet – where you can read accounts of persecution or testimonies of suffering Christians. Neither is this book *statistical*. Again, there are places where people analyse, discuss and sometimes debate the true extent of persecution in different parts of the world today. Rather, this book seeks to bring *biblical* themes to bear on our understanding of persecution – not only because we should care, but also because it is a theme from which we can learn a great deal.

In particular, I want to suggest to you that reflecting biblically on the theme of persecution challenges:

a triumphalist view of our mission;

a consumerist view of our message;

a self-sufficient view of life;

an individualist view of the kingdom; and

a worldly view of hope.

Christians in any age and culture can succumb to some or all of these temptations but we in the West need especially to be aware of them, as we seek to serve Christ in our modern world. We live in, are surrounded by and are influenced by (more than we might care to admit) a culture that *is* triumphalist, consumerist, self-sufficient, individualist and, above all, worldly. To allow the New Testament's teaching on persecution to challenge, mould and transform us in these five areas is actually to be blessed in our faith and to be strengthened and better equipped in our walk with Christ, and in our service of him and his kingdom.

We will, therefore, take each of these themes in turn in the following chapters. As we do so, we will discover that engaging seriously with issues of persecution can help bring biblical truth to bear on our own lives and on the life of our church, as we seek to serve God in our world today.

Chapter 1

Transforming our approach to mission

One of the most profound questions humans can ever ask is also the shortest: "Why?"

This is the question asked by a parent, as they face the funeral of a young child, their emotions utterly shredded and numbed. It is the question we often ask when disaster strikes, and when television news bulletins bring to our living rooms stories of lives being devastated, seemingly without rhyme or reason.

Without doubt, suffering is one of the deepest issues to confront and challenge the faith of believers. It raises big questions about the character of a God who Christians claim is sovereign and almighty – and yet also loving. Does the obvious existence of suffering mean our God can't, or won't, intervene? Those who contribute to the church's mission and witness by writing reasoned defences of the Christian faith (known as apologetics) can scarcely do so without, at some point, attempting to address the huge issue of suffering.

This book is not, however, the place to tackle that broad theme in any deep, philosophical manner. Yet, it is worth acknowledging here that, just as more general forms of suffering can raise tough questions for Christians, so too can the specific form of suffering we are considering: persecution.

We might ask: Why does God allow his people to

suffer for their faith in him? Why is it that those who lovingly seek to share the message of Jesus Christ are sometimes allowed to face hostility, violence, imprisonment – even martyrdom?

Even to begin to think about such matters is challenging, to say the least. We live in a society and culture that seem naturally to magnify and exalt human self-sufficiency, success and triumph. Naturally, we all want to be successful, whether in our chosen career, on the sports field, or in providing for our family. Similarly, as Christians, we will want to see our church grow, outreach to be successful, and mission to flourish. We will want to see the gospel advancing and the faith we profess spreading to all parts of the world. Persecution appears to stand in opposition to all of this. It looks like a form of failure.

Here, then, is the first way that reflecting biblically on the theme of persecution can bless us. It challenges a simplistic, triumphalist view of God's mission in the world and the part we as Christians play in that mission.

Mission and faithfulness

How many of us, I wonder, have ever looked on with a degree of admiration – but with a greater degree of envy and resentment – at that bigger church up the road? The one that appears to have so many resources, that has all the latest mod-cons, that attracts all the young people in the district, and that seems such a success?

Now there's nothing wrong with using the latest technology or being part of a large, thriving church. But the point is this: are those the things we aspire to in mission? And, at the end of the day, are they what give us our peace, our security, and our joy?

The temptation is perhaps more subtle than we would

care to admit, for we live in a competitive, success-driven culture. In sport, in retail, in business, everywhere. The all-pervasive world of advertising constantly coaxes us to yearn for that which is bigger and more luxurious – in short, that which says loudly and clearly that we are a 'success'.

On the night of his arrest, Jesus' disciples were tempted to use all their might to ward off the crowd who had come to seize him. Jesus told them to put away their swords and then added, "Do you think that I cannot appeal to my Father, and that he will at once send me more than twelve legions of angels?" (Matthew 26:53). A 'legion' was generally between 3,000 and 6,000 men in the ancient world. Given how frightening the appearance of just a single angel is in the Bible, this is quite a statement. Jesus was reminding his disciples that he had an almighty, almost incomprehensible power at his disposal – but he was choosing not to use it.

Of course, there will come a day when the Lord's almighty power *will* be seen, when "every knee should bow, in heaven and on earth and under the earth, and every tongue confess that Jesus Christ is Lord" (Philippians 2:10,11). But, in the great and eternal plan of God, that day had not come in the garden of Gethsemane – and has not come yet.

Furthermore, Jesus adds in the next breath, "But how then should the Scriptures be fulfilled...?" (Matthew 26:54). For Jesus, the most important issue in mission was that of faithfulness (in the sense of obedience) to his calling. To the casual observer of that garden scene, Jesus could have appeared vulnerable and weak. All the promise of the previous few years seemed to be coming to a rather lame and disappointing end with an ignominious night-time arrest. At that moment, his disciples may have wanted to voice that profound question, "Why?" Why could he who had healed the sick, miraculously fed a multitude, and even raised the dead not have resisted his enemies and cast them aside?

The answer is that in the apparent weakness and vulnerability of Jesus, a powerful act of God was about to take place. Through the testimony of the Scriptures, we know how the story ends – but we need to keep reminding ourselves of this vital principle. And we Christians in the West, who are seeking to serve the Lord in the midst of our success-oriented society, must keep reminding ourselves of this key mission principle: our sovereign God works out his purposes through weakness and vulnerability.

To engage with, to familiarise ourselves with, and to *identify with* those who are suffering the greatest persecution for Christ is to be reminded of that principle and to see God outworking it in the world today.

In many places where Christians suffer severe persecution, the church is a weak, despised minority, an easy prey for ideological or religious oppressors who are hungry to establish, or to maintain, their own power, privilege and authority. In some cases, the church may be growing – *despite* or *because of* persecution. In other places, the growth may be less evident. To a large extent, growth is not the issue: what we need to focus on is the faithfulness of those serving Christ and his gospel in such a challenging, hostile environment. We should not put them on a pedestal as 'super-Christians', but should recognise that behind their apparent weakness lies the supreme power of God's amazing grace, which continues to be at work in the world and empowers his church in its mission.

That power is seen in the pathetically weak,

imprisoned Christian who, despite cruel and even barbaric treatment, radiates joy and shares the gospel with his fellow prisoners. It is seen in the Christian widow who responds to the slaughter of her family and the destruction of her home by continuing to acknowledge God's goodness and faithfulness. It is seen in the church forced to operate in small, 'underground' cells – yet which continues to worship and witness to Jesus Christ.

Mission and suffering

Jesus wasn't surprised at the events that began to unfold that night in the garden of Gethsemane. During his ministry, he had spoken on several occasions of his coming suffering. In particular, after the Apostle Peter had made that bold, public declaration that Jesus was the promised Messiah, Jesus had begun to teach his disciples where things were heading: "From that time Jesus began to show his disciples that he must go to Jerusalem and suffer many things from the elders and chief priests and scribes, and be killed, and on the third day be raised" (Matthew 16:21). Notice that word, 'must'. This was not gloomy resignation; some kind of reluctant acknowledgement of the writing on the wall. "I can see the way things are panning out here, guys, and, I'm sorry to say, it doesn't look good." No, here was a positive affirmation of his earthly purpose: the Son of Man had come "not to be served but to serve, and to give his life as a ransom for many" (Matthew 20:28). This was his mission. This was why he had come.

We might go even further and say that, at every step of the way, Jesus appeared to be in control, and not just when he was miraculously healing, raising the dead and successfully calling people to follow him. He was in

13

control too *in his time of apparent defeat*. He had taught that he had divine authority to lay down his life and to take it up again (John 10:17,18). In John's account of the arrest, his opponents seem strangely overawed by him (John 18:6) and yet he allows himself to be arrested. Before Pontius Pilate he declares, "You would have no authority over me at all unless it had been given you from above" (John 19:11). In the eyes of the world, this last statement might appear a mere act of human bravado, like the revolutionary who goes to his execution with a resolute and defiant smile on his face. Faith, however, recognises a different, and important, reality here: the sovereign, almighty God is still in control, even though events would suggest otherwise. He is in control as his Son suffers. This later became clear to the Apostle Peter (who famously fled in abject fear at the time of Jesus' arrest) and he alludes to it in the first evangelistic sermon, declaring, "This Jesus, delivered up *according to the definite plan and foreknowledge of God,* you crucified and killed by the hands of lawless men" (Acts 2:23).

Those who live in the crucible of the severest persecution often see this very clearly (by the grace of God), perhaps more clearly than we who live in the comparative freedom of the West. Those of us who have had the immense privilege of visiting, meeting and listening to God's persecuted people around the world are struck by the deep joy and vitality so evident in their faith. They seem less inclined to ask the "Why?" question than we who observe their suffering from a safe distance. They are not masochists. They don't enjoy being persecuted, but they are often acutely aware of God at work in and through their suffering. Yes, we must pray for them. Yes, we can (and ought to) release some of our extensive resources to support and equip them. But they

14

minister to us as they give faithful witness in the midst of suffering.

The Apostle Paul wrote of the Thessalonian Christians, "You became imitators of us and of the Lord, for you received the word in much affliction, with the joy of the Holy Spirit, so that you became an example to all the believers in Macedonia and in Achaia" (1 Thessalonians 1:6,7). He refers to them as an 'example', that is, for the encouragement of other Christians. Persecuted Christians can offer a similar example to us, of faith lived and maintained in the face of affliction and suffering.

Most of us would probably be humble enough to admit we draw encouragement, support and strength from Christian fellowship. The church community that we belong to may not be perfect – and yet we know that, in the long term, there is something very definitely beneficial about being a part of it all.

That being so, it is helpful to recognise the immense value in engaging, in a real and meaningful way, with the lives of persecuted Christians around the world. Their bold witness in adversity challenges our often insipid witness in comfort. Their lives testify to the grace of God that operates in what appears to be human weakness and frailty. This is not an exercise in making ourselves feel guilty, or failures, or hopelessly worldly. It is part of our discipleship – and it is for our blessing.

Mission and the cross

In the breathtaking opening of his letter to the Ephesians, the Apostle Paul declares that "before the foundation of the world" God chose his people to be "in Christ", being redeemed by his blood (that is, by his sacrificial death on the cross). This was, says Paul, all according to the great plan and purpose of God

(Ephesians 1:4-10). In other words, the cross was never God's Plan B. It wasn't a quick-witted piece of divine improvisation, made in response to mankind's shocking and surprising fall into sin. The Scriptures declare to us that *before the foundation of the world* it was God's intention that his eternal Son would come into the world to die for us.

This is hugely significant when it comes to our thinking about suffering. If the cross was, and is, central to God's eternal plan and purpose for his creation, it means that we have a God who always intended to be personally and intimately involved in suffering – and for a purpose.

This does not necessarily answer every philosophical objection to the existence of a sovereign, loving God that suffering might seem to pose. However, it does mean that the incarnation, death and resurrection of Jesus Christ become the place from which the believer can face and respond to the sufferings of this life. The events surrounding the cross seemed to constitute defeat – indeed, humiliating rejection and defeat. But, despite appearances, we know the cross actually spells the greatest victory in all of human history!

That victory over sin and death is the very heartbeat of our faith and has provided the inspiration for countless songs and hymns of adoration, praise and thanksgiving down the centuries. The cross is the ultimate symbol of Christianity – and it is a symbol that speaks of suffering; of God embracing suffering for us. For the persecuted Christian, this adds great dignity to the ordeal of suffering for Christ. The Apostle Peter encouraged first-century Christians who were facing persecution, telling them, "Rejoice insofar as you share Christ's sufferings, that you may also rejoice and be glad when his glory is revealed. If you are insulted for the name of Christ, you are blessed, because the Spirit of glory and of God rests upon you" (1 Peter 4:13,14). We will consider that promise in more detail in a later chapter.

Peter's reference to being insulted is interesting. Very few Christians in the West will have first-hand experience of the more severe forms of persecution suffered by our fellow believers around the world. Yet, many of us may know what it is to be mocked or ridiculed for our faith, perhaps even to provoke irrational anger in a neighbour, friend or relative when we try to share something of our faith in Christ with them.

Persevering in the face of opposition is not about being thick-skinned or heroic. It is not a case of 'when the going gets tough, the tough get going'. Perseverance is a gift of God's grace, given through the one who persevered on our behalf. This is why the writer of the letter to the Hebrews encourages us to continue looking to Jesus who "for the joy that was set before him endured the cross, despising the shame, and is seated at the right hand of the throne of God" (Hebrews 12:2).

This is true for every Christian. But those who have been most tested in the crucible of persecution have probably learnt this lesson better than we who, on the whole, are able to live comparatively comfortably for Christ. Their example is for our blessing – if we take the time and effort to get to know them and their stories.

Mission and the individual's cross

There is, however, a further important dimension to the cross in connection with mission and suffering.

In one very important sense, of course, the cross of Jesus Christ is unique. His sacrifice on the cross was once for all. He, and he alone, was qualified to stand in the

17

place of guilty sinners like us, and to atone for us by bearing the consequences of our sin. Only of Jesus Christ can it be said, "For our sake [God] made him to be sin who knew no sin, so that in him we might become the righteousness of God" (2 Corinthians 5:21). Nothing can be added to the suffering of Christ on the cross, in terms of completing, or somehow making more certain, the eternal salvation that is available in him and through faith in him. It is vital to understand and embrace that.

But, having affirmed the uniqueness of his death in the place of sinners, it is important to recognise that the New Testament writers *also* see in his suffering an example for us to follow. In his encouragement of persecuted Christians, the Apostle Peter writes, "If when you do good and suffer for it you endure, this is a gracious thing in the sight of God. For to this you have been called, because Christ also suffered for you, leaving you an example, so that you might follow in his steps" (1 Peter 2:20-21).

Christ's sufferings provide an example for us to follow in terms of persevering in the face of persecution. But his sufferings do something more: they also provide the model for our ministry and mission. The apparent weakness of Christ that we saw in the garden of Gethsemane should shape the way we approach our mission to the world.

This is something the Apostle Paul emphasises particularly strongly in his two letters to the Corinthian church. Paul's dealings and relationship with the Christian church at Corinth were interesting and complex. The Apostle visited Corinth, it seems, on at least three occasions, including an initial visit (when the church was established) that lasted more than a year and a half (see Acts 18:1-18). In the years that followed, he appears to have written at least four letters to the church there.[1]

Reading between the lines in both New Testament letters, the Christian church in Corinth appeared to have an inflated view of itself. The image people sometimes have, when reading the New Testament today, is that the church in Corinth was a lively and exciting church! In reality, it is clear that the church was both spiritually immature and dangerously worldly in its attitude. It is important to remember this whenever we are reading and studying what Paul has to say to them. Paul seems, at times, to be referring to their spiritual fervour in an almost ironic way, suggesting they were arrogant (eg 1 Corinthians 1:5-7; 2 Corinthians 8:7). But of particular interest to us here is what Paul says about mission.

1 Corinthians 1:18 – 2:5 is a foundational passage in this regard, and one that would repay careful study in relation to the theme of persecution. In these verses, Paul reminds the Corinthians that not only is the content of Christian gospel 'foolish' in the world's eyes, but so too are its messengers *and* the manner in which they are to take that message to the world.

First, the *content*. This is, of course, the cross of our Lord Jesus Christ. The cross, says Paul, "is folly to those who are perishing, but to us who are being saved it is the power of God" (1 Corinthians 1:18). Paul sought to share what Christ had done on the cross with both Jew and non-Jew alike but, he continued, the message of Christ crucified is "a stumbling block to Jews and folly to Gentiles" (1 Corinthians 1:23). The Jews, says Paul,

<hr>

[1] In addition to the two letters we have in our New Testament, Paul refers, in the first of these (1 Corinthians 5:9), to an earlier letter, while in his second letter he recalls a previous letter in which he dealt with a particular issue of discipline (see 2 Corinthians 2:3-9). The subject matter referred to does not seem to accord very easily with 1 Corinthians, suggesting the existence of a letter written at some time between the two letters that have survived.

constantly looked for signs – presumably signs of God's power. The Greeks, on the other hand, were swayed by philosophical wisdom (1 Corinthians 1:22). For both sides, the cross of Christ would appear to fall short. At its heart Christian mission has a message that appears weak and ludicrous in the eyes of the world. That fact is an important one to grasp, if we seek to serve God in this world.

Secondly, there are the *messengers* who deliver that message. Paul writes: "For consider your calling, brothers: not many of you were wise according to worldly standards, not many were powerful, not many were of noble birth. But God chose what is foolish in the world to shame the wise; God chose what is weak in the world to shame the strong. God chose what is low and despised in the world, even things that are not, to bring to nothing things that are, so that no human being might boast in the presence of God" (1 Corinthians 1:26-29). It is interesting to note the make-up of the Christian church in cosmopolitan Corinth! Paul's point, however, is not that God has no use for you in Christian mission if you are rich, powerful and intellectual! Rather, it is important to recognise that you don't *have to be* any of these things in order to be used by God in the effective service of his kingdom. And that, of course, runs counter to what the world generally considers necessary to be able to succeed. "Might is right," and "Money talks," so it is said.

But then, thirdly, there is the *method* employed by the messengers. They are, quite simply, to preach the gospel. At several points in this passage, Paul emphasises this (1 Corinthians 1:17, 21, 23; 1 Corinthians 2:1, 4). As he does so, he contrasts his methodology with what he calls 'wisdom'. Now, we need to be careful not to misunderstand Paul in this. Paul is not saying he spoke gibberish, nor is he making some kind of anti-intellectual jibe. To contrast his gospel ministry with worldly wisdom certainly does not mean that Paul was *simplistic* or *trite*. Paul was, after all, a man of great intellect himself – and God used that intellect very effectively, in his preaching and teaching. No, what Paul is doing is contrasting the Christian task of preaching and explaining what Christ did on the cross with the kind of worldly, philosophical wisdom – dressed up, no doubt, in great artistic and presentational skill – that, sadly, seemed to impress the Christians in Corinth. As Paul emphasises: "And I, when I came to you, brothers, did not come proclaiming to you the testimony of God with lofty speech or wisdom. For I decided to know nothing among you except Jesus Christ and him crucified" (1 Corinthians 2:1,2).

The church in the West would do well to heed this teaching – for we live in a world where outward form and 'show' often tend to count for so much. Ours is, increasingly, a culture driven by the obsessive desire to be entertained. Sadly, these characteristics are sometimes present in the church. Paul, by contrast, was happy to declare to these Corinthians: "I was with you in weakness and in fear and much trembling, and my speech and my message were not in plausible words of wisdom, but in demonstration of the Spirit and of power, that your faith might not rest in the wisdom of men but in the power of God" (1 Corinthians 2:3-5). The power that Paul refers to here is not the sort of power that impresses the world. Nor is it something we can whip up or manipulate ourselves, by our cleverness, by our wisdom, by creating a certain 'atmosphere' at a meeting, or by our ability as speakers to perform. It is God's power, God taking the simple presentation of the gospel and using it – as and when he chooses – to turn people's lives around.

And it is those parts of God's church that are facing the severest forms of persecution today that often appear to embody this teaching most clearly. For very often the situation in which they find themselves means they have very little of the world's power or resources or advantages at their disposal. The gospel is not presented in the latest glossy packaging: it is shared by people who, carrying nothing more than a Bible (and sometimes not even that), tell others about Jesus. And even if it brings immense suffering, they continue to do so.

On a visit to India, I met a pastor who was from a Hindu priestly background. When he came to faith in Christ, his family, and the rest of the villagers where he lived, opposed him and tried to force him to return to Hinduism. When he refused, he was beaten up and thrown out of the village. He was left with nothing but the clothes he was wearing. Some Christian friends, however, supported him and later helped pay for him to train at Bible college. When he finished his training, he went back to his home village to share the gospel. Again, he was opposed by Hindu extremists, who threatened to destroy his home and who called in the local police, accusing him of forcing and bribing people to become Christians.

This man had nothing with which to impress others outwardly. But he had the gospel. And people began to respond – including his own father, who had at first bitterly opposed him. Such testimonies are a powerful witness to the sovereign work of God and a reminder to us of this important mission principle of God's power at work in and through human weakness.

By the time Paul came to write his second letter to the Corinthians, the Apostle's relationship with them had become more problematic. It seems the church had fallen under the sway of a group of itinerant preachers. Determining exactly who they were, and the nature of the trouble they were causing, are key factors in studying, understanding and applying 2 Corinthians (as reference to any commentary on the letter makes apparent). On the one hand, it seems these itinerants were of Jewish origin (see 2 Corinthians 11:22). On the other hand, the issues their activity raised were not specifically Jewish. There is no suggestion, for example, that they were insisting on Gentile Christians adopting the outward practices of Judaism (which Paul had encountered earlier in his ministry and had had to deal with quite forcefully in his letter to the Galatians). In fact, the problems they were causing do not seem to be fundamentally theological or doctrinal at all.

Rather, they appeared to be people who emphasised and boasted of outward power and strength. They set great store by their reputation (2 Corinthians 3:1; 2 Corinthians 10:12), by their powerful oratory and knowledge (2 Corinthians 11:6) and by the impact they had. They lorded it over those they won over (2 Corinthians 11:20), and may have been boasting about possessing miraculous power (2 Corinthians 12:12). Moreover, they were denigrating the Apostle Paul's ministry – because, outwardly, his ministry seemed to lack these things. Paul was not, in their eyes, an impressive speaker, although – they claimed – he liked to give that impression in his letters (2 Corinthians 10:10). They may have been maligning him because he had won few of his own people (the Jews) with his gospel message (2 Corinthians 4:3-4).

The crux of the matter is perhaps found in Paul's reference to "those who boast about outward appearance and not about what is in the heart" (2 Corinthians 5:12).

Despite the apparent lack of doctrinal issues, it is questionable whether we can even call the ministry of this group genuinely Christian. Paul, somewhat sarcastically, refers to them as "super-Apostles" (2 Corinthians 11:5; 2 Corinthians 12:11). He questions their sincerity (2 Corinthians 2:17), and implies they manipulate their message in order to gain a following (2 Corinthians 4:2). Most pointedly, he refers to their message as "a different gospel" (2 Corinthians 11:4).

If we are brutally honest with ourselves, it is not difficult to picture these people – or to understand how easily the Corinthians had been won over by them. We see their attitude in some sections of the Western church today, where much is invested in what is big and impressive and powerful. Most Christians might be quick to reject the obvious excesses of the 'health, wealth and prosperity' movements, and yet we can be drawn to those things that appear outwardly powerful and impressive in more subtle ways. Committing to a small, local fellowship may be unattractive, compared with travelling a few miles to be part of something bigger and more exciting. The faithful, expository preaching and teaching of God's word can sometimes rank a poor second – both for believers' discipleship and for outreach to unbelievers – to the desire to be entertained and amused.

Paul's response to what we might call the worldly triumphalism of his opponents is noteworthy. Although, towards the end of the letter, he does engage in some ironic boasting of his own (particularly in chapter 12), he does not attempt to compete with them, particularly in those areas where they have been most critical of him and his ministry. He does not, for example, set out to impress by citing a list of the churches he had established (as he could so easily have done). So how does Paul respond in

2 Corinthians? He responds by pointing to his *weakness and suffering*.

It is in his suffering for the cause of the gospel that Paul is identified with Christ (2 Corinthians 1:5), for Christ himself – as we have seen – appeared weak and suffered. Yes, there is power in mission, but it is God's power in God's gospel (2 Corinthians 4:5-6). God's people, who have been given the task of proclaiming that gospel to the world will, by contrast, appear weak – and may well be prey to the powerful and persecuting forces of the world. In fact, if we had to sum up the central theme of Paul's argument in 2 Corinthians, it would be 'God's power that is manifest in human weakness'. Paul states this contrast beautifully: "But we have this treasure [the gospel] in jars of clay, to show that the surpassing power belongs to God and not to us" (2 Corinthians 4:7). Clay pottery was the everyday material of ordinary people in the ancient world. Such are those who proclaim the gospel of Jesus Christ to the world: ordinary – and even fragile! Why? That we might know, and remember, that the power to transform lives comes from God, and not from us. While his opponents boasted of their 'success' and strength, Paul's CV is characterised by suffering and weakness *through which* God works (2 Corinthians 4:8-9; 2 Corinthians 6:4-10; 2 Corinthians 11:22-33).

Christians, as Paul goes on to say, are ambassadors for Christ (what a noble title!) and through us God makes his appeal to the world, to be reconciled to him through the sacrificial, saving work of his Son (2 Corinthians 5:18-20). But we exercise this ambassadorial role not with outward displays of power and influence (for we are not trying to win people over by impressing them), but by trusting in the Lord, by preaching his gospel and by being willing to suffer for him. Indeed, according to Paul, this is how service to God is commended (2 Corinthians 6:4-5; 2 Corinthians 11:24-27). It is from this perspective that Paul can sum up his approach to mission by declaring, "Therefore I will boast all the more gladly of my weaknesses, so that the power of Christ may rest upon me. For the sake of Christ then, I am content with weaknesses, insults, hardships, persecutions, and calamities. For when I am weak, then I am strong" (2 Corinthians 12:9-10). For Paul, the true apostolic life was marked by hardship, danger and persecution – not by personal acclaim.

In short, as he seeks to counter the influence of the glitzy visitors to Corinth, Paul promotes a lifestyle characterised, above all, by weakness (2 Corinthians 4:5; 2 Corinthians 13:4).

Here is a radical blueprint for mission that runs counter to so much that we hear from the world around us, particularly in the West. I am not suggesting that we have *nothing* to learn from the world today, in terms of good practices, of training, of how to run Christian organisations and so on. But in Christian mission our trust is ultimately not in self, our creativity, ingenuity and marketing prowess, but in the Lord.

That last sentence seems so obvious that we might be tempted to dismiss it as a mere truism; but I would suggest we need to go on hearing it, as we need to go on hearing the teaching of the Apostle Paul.

If that is the case, there is a sense in which we might say we simply need to go on reading (and heeding) our Bibles. At times, however, it is good to see the truth of Scripture earthed in the world around us. Preachers, for example, will often illustrate the truths they are teaching with stories, or with quotes from Christian writers. Where the church is living through severe persecution today, the New Testament's teaching on suffering for Christ and the gospel, and on God's power manifest in weakness, is indeed earthed, tangibly and visibly. Faith – total dependence on God that he will use the simple, unadorned preaching of the gospel to build his kingdom – is plain to see in the lives of his suffering people. Their witness, their enthusiastic mission, exercised in apparent weakness – and often through suffering – is a challenging reminder to us of the principles we see the Apostle Paul emphasising.

For us in the West to engage with persecution, reflecting on it biblically, and making it a central theme in our understanding of the Christian life, can help us to view mission in a more God-centred way. The New Testament model for ministry and mission is one of self-sacrifice and apparent weakness: "We are treated as imposters, and yet are true; as unknown, and yet well known; as dying, and behold, we live; as punished, and yet not killed; as sorrowful, yet always rejoicing; as poor, yet making many rich; as having nothing, yet possessing everything" (2 Corinthians 6:8-10).

To embrace this is to hear and obey the call of Jesus himself, who told his disciples, "If anyone would come after me, let him deny himself and *take up his cross* and follow me" (Matthew 16:24). When persecution has little or no place in our thinking about the Christian life, it is tempting (as we suggested in the Introduction) to water down such words, and to apply them quite broadly and generally to any form of hardship or misfortune that may come our way in life. "That's the cross I have to bear" is a common phrase, and one applied to everything from a chronic back problem to having a house full of wayward teenagers!

But, moments before Jesus spoke about our cross, he had begun to teach his disciples about *his* cross (Matthew 16:21); to 'take up *our* cross' is to be willing to suffer for him and for the gospel. To be willing to suffer – and to die – for *him*.

Interestingly, between Jesus' cross and our cross we hear Peter attempting to dissuade Jesus from following this path: "Far be it from you, Lord! This shall never happen to you" (Matthew 16:22). At this point in the story, there was no place for suffering in Peter's understanding of the Messiah and his mission. As a Jew, Peter understood the Messiah's coming as an event that would immediately usher in the final earthly and visible victory of God over his enemies. His words, however, are met with a stinging rebuke from Jesus: "Get behind me, Satan! You are a hindrance to me. For you are not setting your mind on the things of God, but on the things of man" (Matthew 16:23). The Messiah's coming was, indeed, to secure the full and final victory of God over sin and death – but the path to that victory was marked by suffering.

The "things of man" rather than the "things of God" was Jesus' description of Peter's attitude. It would be an apt way to sum up the mindset of those "super-Apostles" in Corinth to whom Paul was responding. It would be an apt way to sum up a triumphalist view of Christian mission. Or a view of the Christian life that gives little or no thought to the theme of persecution, and of living with human weakness by the grace of God.

Persecution challenges a simplistic, triumphalist view of Christian mission. Acknowledging its reality and reflecting on it biblically points us to the God who works out his sovereign purposes – who carries out *his* mission – in and through human weakness. This was true in the life and work of Jesus Christ, as we see so clearly at the cross, and it is true in the mission to which he calls Christ's followers. Engaging with the persecution of God's people in our world today can, therefore, be a real blessing to us as we embrace the call to mission in a more God-centred way.

But what is it about the Christian gospel itself that should make us see suffering and persecution as inevitable in mission? It is to that question that we will turn in the next chapter.

Your response

1. Read 2 Corinthians 4. What can we learn about God's mission and our part in that mission? What light does this chapter of the Bible shed on the issue of persecution?
2. "Our sovereign God works out his purposes through weakness and vulnerability." How does that statement affect your thinking about church mission?
3. What might it mean to follow the example of Christ in our mission to the world?

Chapter 2

Sharpening our understanding of the gospel

W e live in a consumerist world. And in that world, "the customer is always right," or – even if he isn't – he is at least a force to be reckoned with.

So what do you do, in that context, if you are struggling as a 'retailer' or 'provider'? If your business is not growing in the way you would want? If you are not a success? Well, naturally, you look to change something: perhaps your logo, perhaps the way you market your product, or the target audience for your advertising.

In the consumerist world, rebranding is serious stuff. Business gurus write endless reams of copy about good and bad lessons to be learnt from rebranding. Pay attention to what the public says and respond. Use slogans that tell customers you are adapting to meet their needs and demands, and so on. So a fast-food chain attempts to broaden its appeal by putting out a new advert about its coffee... A struggling technology brand creates a new slim-line product in beautiful packaging and sparks a global revolution.

And then, of course, there is the church.

The church has a mission, just as every business has a mission. The church's mission is, in the words of its founder, to "go and make disciples of all nations" (Matthew 28:19). So what does the church do if its mission seems to be struggling, if it isn't growing, if in fact it is in decline? Herein lies the danger.

One temptation for the church (and particularly, I would suggest, for the church in the West) is to follow the world's lead: to focus on techniques and marketing strategies that are appealing and attractive. This is not to deny the value of being culturally relevant and accessible. Nor is it to question the value of providing programmes that help the church connect with people locally, or which meet perceived community needs. Far from it. The church needs to know how to engage with the world on its doorstep. But the church in the West needs reminding that at the heart of our mission is a message that the world will, by nature, *reject*. And that doesn't mean the message is therefore wrong. It doesn't mean we need to rebrand it. We certainly don't need to soften its edges to make it more palatable. And it is important that we understand why not.

In the last chapter, we noted that those immature Christians at Corinth seemed impressed by those who had a worldly way of doing things, and who measured mission and success in worldly terms. In his second letter to that church, Paul, by contrast, says of his own ministry: "We refuse to practise cunning or to tamper with God's word, but by the open statement of the truth we would commend ourselves to everyone's conscience in the sight of God" (2 Corinthians 4:2). He goes on to say in the next verse that if people reject that message it is because "the god of this world" (Satan) has blinded them. Paul's 'carry on regardless' approach to his mission task and to the message he presented would not go down too well with modern marketing gurus! It is an approach, however, that is rooted, not in stubbornness or in an arrogant confidence in his own resources and ability, but in an attitude that is willing to trust results to the sovereign grace of God.

And so we come to the second way that reflecting biblically on the theme of persecution can be a blessing to us. It challenges a consumerist view of our message and in doing so sharpens our understanding of the true gospel.

Persecution of the church

What will we discover if we seek to learn about the persecuted church – in China, India, Iran, Pakistan, Nigeria or so many other places around the world?

We will see a church that is often despised, that frequently suffers, but that remains faithful to Christ and that continues to preach the gospel – the very gospel that causes it to be so despised.

It is not a perfect church, of course. Such a thing doesn't exist. The purpose of this book is not to encourage you to idolise the persecuted church, the way a sports fan might idolise a favourite team or player. The purpose is to see that engaging with persecution, and identifying with, supporting and praying for persecuted Christians, is not only our responsibility but is also something that will bless us and our churches.

As we begin to discover what is happening to Christians around the world, we are bound to ask, What is it about Christianity that provokes such reactions? What are people afraid of? Christians have a message that we describe as 'good news' (that is the meaning of the word 'gospel'). Generally speaking, Christians tend to be peace-loving people and good citizens. So what is it about the Christian gospel that provokes such antagonism?

Jesus clearly taught his disciples to expect this sort of reaction. At one point in his earthly ministry, he sent his disciples out on what might be described as a prototype, training mission. In doing so, he warned them, "Behold, I am sending you out as sheep in the midst of wolves, so be wise as serpents and innocent as doves. Beware of men, for they will deliver you over to courts and flog you in their synagogues" (Matthew 10:16-17). And it gets worse! He continues: "Brother will deliver brother over to death, and the father his child, and children will rise against parents and have them put to death, and you will be hated by all for my name's sake" (Matthew 10:21-22). As recruiting pitches go, this is hardly inspiring. Shouldn't Jesus have emphasised the positives a bit more?

There is, however, a sobering reality to what Jesus says. In many Muslim-majority countries today, for example, if a person comes to faith in Christ – from a Muslim background – the biggest threat to them often comes from those closest to them: associates, friends or even members of their own family.

I know of a former Islamic cleric in Pakistan who came to faith in Christ. When word spread that he had become a Christian, he had to flee his home. His wife filed a suit in a family court that meant he did not see his children for three years. Those who had formerly been his friends now wanted to take his life. Some time later, by God's grace, his wife came to faith and they were reunited. But living for Christ continued to mean living in hiding from his former colleagues.

There is also a deep spiritual truth in Jesus' words. His warnings remind us what a radical message the Christian gospel is. Yes, it is good news – the greatest news, in fact – for it offers God's mercy and forgiveness. It declares we can know God for ourselves, and assures us of eternal life in his glorious presence. But to speak of mercy and forgiveness is at once to be reminded of our sin and failure. The gospel invitation is to come to Jesus: to come as we are, but recognising that we are sinners – which means we must come in repentance and faith, accepting Jesus' right to be the Lord of our lives.

To see it in these terms is to be reminded that the Christian gospel is, therefore, deeply insulting to human pride and self-centredness. Only by God's grace will anyone accept it. When the church loses sight of this, it runs the risk of following the world in its mission practices, of trying desperately to convince outsiders that joining the Christian church will bring them happiness, fun and friendship with genuinely nice people who believe in God. It may do that, of course – and more – but that is not the gospel.

In the West, the church, by and large, lives under the protection of a culture, and of laws, with Judeo-Christian roots. That has meant that, while you might be mocked for your Christian faith, you are unlikely to have your home destroyed because of it – and you wouldn't expect to be imprisoned for it. In other parts of the world, the setting is very different for the Christian church. Where the prevailing culture – and sometimes even the law of the land – permits it, society has freer rein to express its reaction to that 'insulting' Christian gospel.

Hatred of Jesus

The night before he was crucified, Jesus spent his time, at the Last Supper, teaching his disciples (John 13-16) and praying in the light of that teaching (John 17). Jesus looks beyond his death, resurrection and ascension to the period in which we are now living, the period between his first coming, as Suffering Servant, and his return, as glorious Lord and Judge. His message focuses on what it will mean for his disciples to serve him in the world, coupled with the fact that Jesus will be with them, through the gift and presence of the Holy Spirit.

His followers are to remember that he is the only way to the Father. They are to remain faithful to him, and to demonstrate to the world that they belong to Jesus by the love they show one another.

And if they do these things, the world is likely to *hate* them.

"If the world hates you, know that it has hated me before it hated you. If you were of the world, the world would love you as its own; but because you are not of the world, but I chose you out of the world, therefore the world hates you" (John 15:18-19). If we are honest, these are not words that we find it easy to hear and to accept. We don't welcome the thought that someone hates us. Rejection, whether expressed aggressively or apathetically, is an uncomfortable experience – which is, perhaps, one reason why so many of us find evangelism so difficult.

In John's Gospel, the word "world" is frequently used to refer to those who are manifestly rejecting Jesus. Jesus is saying that hatred shown to Christians is, in effect, the expression of a hatred of Jesus himself. When Christians are persecuted, the world is demonstrating what it thinks of Jesus.

When Christians are living for Jesus, and proclaiming him to the world, the world is confronted by the challenging message of the gospel; by that call to come to Jesus as Saviour and Lord. We shouldn't be surprised that the world, preferring to remain in its sinful rebellion, will reject that message. At times – and when it has the opportunity to do so – the world will reject that message violently.

We see an example of this hatred of Jesus being

expressed towards his followers in the early life of the Apostle Paul. While still the zealous Pharisee Saul, he was at the forefront of those who opposed this new 'sect'. We first meet him in the story of Stephen's martyrdom where it is said he looked after the garments of those who carried out the stoning and that he approved of what happened (Acts 7:58-Acts 8:1).

Soon afterwards, Saul himself takes a lead in attacking followers of Jesus. However, on the road to Damascus – where he was intending to have more of them arrested – he is stopped in his tracks by a vision of the resurrected Lord. And what is it that Jesus says to him? "Saul, Saul, why are you persecuting *me*?" (Acts 9:4). Not, "Why are you persecuting my followers?" but "Why are you persecuting me?" Jesus is making an important point: Saul's attitude and actions are a rejection of Jesus himself. "I am Jesus, whom you are persecuting," says the Lord, pointedly (Acts 9:5).

To become a follower of Jesus, and to live as a follower of Jesus, is hardly a good way to make yourself popular with the world. As we have already seen, Jesus declared, "If you were of the world, the world would love you as its own; but because you are not of the world, but I chose you out of the world, therefore the world hates you" (John 15:19). This doesn't mean, of course, that non-Christians all love each other, get on wonderfully with each other and only dislike Christians: we only need to read our newspapers or watch the daily news bulletins on television to know that hatred and enmity are widespread and complex. But the point is that, wherever and whenever Christians are being faithful to Christ, they will stand out from the crowd. In fact, to change the analogy, they will find themselves 'swimming against the tide'. To 'go with the flow' is far easier – but not the best thing to do if you want to get to the other side! As we said earlier, the gospel is a radical, challenging message, one that is insulting to human pride and which people will, by nature, reject. This reality is illustrated powerfully in John's Gospel by the vivid image of light and darkness. "Again Jesus spoke to them, saying, 'I am the light of the world. Whoever follows me will not walk in darkness, but will have the light of life'" (John 8:12). In his prologue, John describes Jesus as the "true light" which has come into the world – and yet, he tells us, the world did not know him or receive him (John 1:9-11). Why? A little later we are told. "And this is the judgement: the light has come into the world, and people loved the darkness rather than the light because their works were evil" (John 3:19).

If someone were to shine a powerful torch at you, particularly in a darkened room, your natural reaction would be to avert your eyes, or to shield them from the light. This is, in effect, the natural reaction of the sinful human nature to Jesus. "For everyone who does wicked things hates the light and does not come to the light, lest his works should be exposed" (John 3:20). The light that wonderfully reveals God (John 1:18) also disturbs those who reject him.

Ignorance of God

Rejecting Jesus, the natural default reaction of human beings, is serious because he came to reveal God – indeed, to reconcile us to God.

The world's hatred of Christians, Jesus says, is a reflection of their hatred – and rejection – of him. He continues: "But all these things they will do to you on account of my name, *because they do not know him who sent me*" (John 15:21).

So when the world persecutes Christians, it is expressing its rejection of the Christ that Christians represent. Those 'of the world' want nothing to do with the Christ who shines a holy light into their sinful hearts, and who calls them to receive him as their Lord. *And in so doing*, the world expresses its ignorance of the one true God – for Jesus Christ is the only way to God (John 14:6, John 1:18).

Jesus' logical – and chilling – conclusion is: "Whoever hates me *hates my Father also*" (John 15:23). The persecution of Christians is a graphic reminder to us of mankind's sinful nature which exists in ignorance of God. It is good to be reminded of this because only when we truly understand human nature, as it is presented to us by God in Scripture, will we understand why and how the gospel of Jesus Christ meets mankind's deepest and most significant need.

Sometimes, when confronted by the reality – and severity – of persecution around the world, Christians in the West are often surprised. But why? We should not be surprised if we have a truly biblical understanding of both human nature and of the gospel – for neither have changed.

As we suggested earlier, persecution – suffering for Christ and his gospel – is a central theme in New Testament teaching. Therefore, reflecting biblically on persecution, engaging with its existence today in a real and meaningful way is good for us, for it drives us back to Scripture and to the gospel. It sharpens our understanding of the message we are to proclaim to the world.

Opposition of Satan

As well as preserving the teaching Jesus gave to his

disciples at the Last Supper, John also records the prayer Jesus prayed, shortly before his arrest (John 17). In this prayer, the contrast between his followers and the world is once again prominent (for example, in verses 6, 9 and 11), and then Jesus prays: "I have given them your word, and the world has hated them because they are not of the world, just as I am not of the world. I do not ask that you take them out of the world, but that you keep them from the *evil one*" (John 17:14-15).

Jesus' words remind us of a third dimension to persecution that sharpens our thinking about the gospel. We have seen that it reflects a hatred of Jesus, whose light exposes the sinful nature of our hearts, and we have seen that this in turn testifies to mankind's ignorance of God. But it is also important to remember there is an evil one who seeks to oppose God's plans and purposes in the world. That means, ultimately, that he seeks to oppose the gospel. And the persecution of God's church is one way he attempts to do this.

The dramatic visions given to John, and which he recorded in the Book of Revelation, are a reminder of this. In chapter 12 of Revelation, the curtain is pulled back, as it were, to reveal the spiritual warfare that surrounded the coming of Jesus Christ into the world, the central event in all human history. The dragon (identified in Revelation 12:9 as Satan) seeks to devour the child who will "rule the nations" (Revelation 12:5). This, we are told in Scripture, has been his aim from the beginning. After mankind's original act of rebellion – instigated by Satan's temptation – we read, in Genesis, God's declaration to the serpent: "I will put enmity between you and the woman and between your offspring and her offspring; he shall bruise your head, and you shall bruise his heel" (Genesis 3:15). In John's vision, the child escapes the dragon's clutches and is "caught up to God and to his throne" (Revelation 12:5). This is seen as the decisive battle, at the end of which the dragon is "thrown down to the earth" (Revelation 12:13; see also Jesus' comments in John 12:31).

But, although defeated at the cross, the evil one is not yet finally destroyed. That day is still to come. In the meantime, John's vision tells us, "Then the dragon became furious with the woman and went off to make war on the rest of her offspring, on those who keep the commandments of God and hold to the testimony of Jesus" (Revelation 12:17). Satan seeks to thwart, and to bring down, the church of Jesus Christ.

This should not alarm us, or terrify us, or cause us to look for satanic activity around every corner. The Book of Revelation is, after all, written to encourage Christians! At the same time, though, the passage we have been considering, and The Book of Revelation as a whole, cause us to see life from a different perspective – a spiritual and eternal perspective. The opposition that the church will face in the world is painted boldly in the book's symbolic language – and yet so is the final victory that belongs to Christ. In the same vision, John tells us that God's people have overcome Satan "by the blood of the Lamb and by the word of their testimony for they loved not their lives even unto death" (Revelation 12:11). As always, our victory is in and through the sacrificial death of Jesus Christ on our behalf. And, once again, we see that persecution is bound up with belonging to Jesus, and with the gospel we proclaim.

So, where's all the persecution?

At this point it is worth pausing to consider a question that often arises when Christians in the West begin thinking seriously about issues of persecution: Why don't we see more of it in the West? It is a fair question, but one we need to handle with care, for it can easily become a *loaded* question, presupposing some inherent failure on the part of the Western church. Surely – so the thought goes – if we don't see the same persecution that the church is experiencing in other parts of the world, it must be because we are doing something very wrong?

There are some key points to note here. They need to be born in mind together, as part of a bigger picture, rather than being seen as alternatives.

First, it is helpful to understand what we mean by 'persecution' or by the concept of suffering for Christ and for being his followers. Although the New Testament records the martyrdom and imprisonment of Christians, it also speaks of insult and mockery when referring to our suffering for Christ. As we noted earlier, Christians in the West may not, at present, be witnessing or experiencing some of the more severe forms of persecution, but we may well know what it is to be reviled, insulted or spoken against for holding on to a robust, biblical faith in Christ. Understandably, it is easy to feel guilty – or weak – for referring to 'insults' as persecution, as Christians in other parts of the world are imprisoned for years, beaten up or even killed for being identified with Jesus Christ and the gospel. Nevertheless, it is helpful to recognise and acknowledge the spectrum of suffering for Christ that is referred to in the Scriptures.

Secondly, it is important to appreciate that Christianity has sunk deep roots into Western society and culture, partly as a result of God blessing gospel ministry and witness down the centuries. For this, we ought to be thankful. The impact of Christianity on the Western world is a huge subject all of its own, and we cannot dwell on it here. However, as Western society broadly and generally embraced Christian morals and attitudes (which does not necessarily mean biblical faith in every individual) so, over a long period of time, a culture has developed in which the church and Christianity have been accepted as an essential part of that society. It is not difficult to see that this acceptance has inevitably provided the church with some protection from assault – at least physical attack.

In fact, the acceptance and embracing of broadly Christian morals and attitudes has arguably been a major factor in the general stability of society in the Western world. Why is it, for example, that a state such as the United Kingdom has not witnessed a succession of military coups in its recent history? Social historians might wish to discuss that at length, but I would suggest that a thorough, honest answer would have to factor in the long-term influence of Protestant Christianity and Christian values. The modern breed of aggressive atheists would do well to ponder what kind of society they might be creating as they seek to marginalise Christianity and to exclude it from the public realm.

Thirdly, and this is in some sense the flip-side to the previous point, two of the major human 'drivers' of severe persecution elsewhere are absent in the West: namely, totalitarian government (particularly of the Communist variety) and the more extremist forms of other religions. These have not existed with sufficient power or in sufficient number in the West to be able to confront Christianity as they might in other parts of the world.

Finally, and notwithstanding all that has just been said, we shouldn't dismiss entirely the self-criticism implied in the original question. Where Christians in the West know *nothing* of what it means to be mocked for Christ, to be rejected or abused for Christ, or just to be made to feel strange, weird or unwelcome – because of their allegiance to Christ – one has to question the credibility or reality of their Christian witness.

From time to time, we hear secular politicians in the West commending the church for its involvement in community welfare or its participation in some aspect of social justice. That's great, from both angles. On the one hand, it is right and good that Christians care about all people. The Christian church has a long and noble history of demonstrating Christian love in tangible ways that seek to make a positive difference in people's lives – and long may it continue to do so. Also, it is understandable, and appropriate, that politicians should acknowledge the contribution *any* institution makes to the good of the wider community.

But that same secular politician is unlikely to be so approving of the church for preaching the gospel of the cross and calling on all people to come to Jesus Christ in repentance and faith (which is the prime mission task of the church). In fact (depending on his own beliefs – or lack of them), he might be quite insulted by it. The point is not that we should care less about social justice and providing for the needy, but that we should care *more* about proclaiming the gospel of the cross – even though it will not win us the same plaudits. On the contrary, spreading the gospel will inevitably bring opposition. And given that most of us probably prefer being commended to being attacked, it is not difficult to recognise the temptation to shy away from preaching the cross.

In his letter to the Galatians, the Apostle Paul defended the message of the cross and God's grace in the face of those who sought to make Christians conform to mere 'outward' religion (in this case the outward rituals of Judaism). This would, said Paul, remove "the offence of the cross" (Galatians 5:11). Towards the end of the letter, he adds: "It is those who want to make a good showing in the flesh who would force you to be circumcised, and only in order that they may not be persecuted for the cross of Christ" (Galatians 6:12). Tempting, indeed. "But far be it from me to boast except in the cross of our Lord Jesus Christ, by which the world has been crucified to me, and I to the world," he adds (Galatians 6:14).

All of this is a further reminder of how we can learn from persecuted Christians around the world, and how our engaging with them, finding out about them and hearing their stories can be a blessing to us. As we've mentioned, they very often display a zeal for sharing the gospel – indeed, an urgency to do so – that is lacking in the West. Their discipleship and witness, lived out in the cauldron of severe persecution, can challenge, motivate and encourage us in our own service of Christ and of his gospel.

In this chapter we have been reminded of the two fundamental *spiritual* reasons why Christians are persecuted: First, the sinful human nature, which rejects the claims of Christ and, second, the activity of Satan, who seeks to oppose the gospel.

To focus on the spiritual reasons is not to invalidate, or to contradict, any analysis of persecution that concentrates on the human motives and causes. Political ideology, aggressive religious fundamentalism and the desire to maintain a certain culture or way of life are all reasons why Christians are persecuted in our world today. In the Book of Acts it is clear that on two occasions the reasons were financial: the impact of the gospel threatened people's profit-making (Acts 16:16-24, and Acts 19:23-29)!

Analysing the various human motives for persecution is helpful, for it shows us what it is like to live as a follower of Jesus Christ in different parts of our world today. And the more we understand the conditions in which our fellow Christians are living, the more we will be motivated to pray for them, and the better equipped we will be to know how best to care for them.

An example of this is Richard Wurmbrand, the inspiration behind the founding of Release International. Wurmbrand was a Romanian Lutheran pastor who, from the late 1940s, suffered a total of 14 years' imprisonment, as a result of his gospel ministry, at the hands of his country's Communist authorities. During that time, he regularly endured torture and isolation, in appalling conditions. After his second release from prison, he was ransomed out of the country, and embarked on a significant international ministry: telling the Christian church in the West his story – and opening people's eyes to what Christians were suffering at the hands of Communists behind the Iron Curtain. His testimony shone a clear light on the atheistic agenda and attitudes of Communism – and, in particular, its blind, rabid fear of 'religious' people who give their first allegiance not to the state, but to their God. Christians in the West were then better equipped to respond, pray for and care for their Christian brothers and sisters living in Communist countries.

But the deeper, spiritual reasons that we have focused on in this chapter lie behind, and help explain, the various human motives that drive people to persecute Christians. Furthermore, they serve to sharpen our understanding of the gospel as God's answer to mankind's deepest needs.

These first two chapters, dealing as they have done with the church's mission and with the gospel message it is to proclaim, are closely bound up together. As we explore what we can learn from persecution, it becomes clear that there is an unmistakable, and perhaps even uncomfortable, vulnerability about Christian mission. We have a message that appears weak and foolish to the world. The world, when being faithful to its own nature, will reject that message because it is a message that confronts the world with the One who exposes its sin. And yet, in contrast to the world's way of doing things – which often involves adapting one's message and the presentation of that message in order to be more attractive – we have been reminded that the church is to remain faithful to the task of preaching the gospel. We are to do so trusting that God will do the work that only God can do: that of bringing people out of spiritual darkness into the light of Christ.

When we allow ourselves to be informed about the persecuted church, that vulnerability becomes apparent. This may be why we may shy away from engaging deeply with issues of persecution, despite what Scripture may say to us about the importance of doing so. Weakness and vulnerability are, after all, rarely vote-winners in our culture. We would rather dwell on things that emphasise joy and happiness and that create a general feeling of well-being about our Christian lives or about our church.

However, as we have seen during the course of these first two chapters, Christ-like mission is carried out with the willingness to appear weak and foolish in the eyes of the world, and with the faith that God builds his kingdom through the faithful preaching of a gospel that also appears weak, foolish and, indeed, insulting.

47

Vulnerability will always be something of a hallmark of the persecuted church. It is a vulnerability that is content with weakness, insult and hardship because it relies on the sovereign grace of God – not on the ingenuity and skill of human presentation – to bring people to faith. It is to that grand theme that we turn in more detail in the next chapter.

Your response

1. Read John 15:18 – John 16:4. Imagine you were present at the Last Supper when Jesus spoke these words. How would you feel about the task of telling the world about him?
2. How does the persecution of Christians help us understand better both human nature and the Christian gospel?
3. Is it easier to get involved in social welfare than to tell others about Jesus? If so, why?

Chapter 3

Deepening our desire for grace

Question: "Why did Moses spend forty years wandering in the desert?" Answer: "Because men never ask for directions."

Men never ask for directions? Have you heard that old quip? How many exasperated wives have been tempted to repeat it during a prolonged and frustrating car journey?

The implication behind the sentiment seems to be that asking for directions would puncture manly pride. Having a sense of direction is – like DIY – something men believe they are inherently good at. Needing to ask for directions is, therefore, a blow to the ego.

Now, regardless of how accurate that caricature of the male psyche may or may not be, pride in our own ability or self-sufficiency is certainly a dangerous thing – and I'm not just talking about geography.

The Christian gospel challenges human self-sufficiency. In fact, it totally pulls the rug out from under it! For the gospel declares that Jesus came to meet our deepest, most desperate need. And, more importantly, he came to do what we could not do for ourselves.

Jesus' earthly mission was not just to give us a helping hand or to point us in the right direction, that we might then find our way to God and to life eternal by our own efforts, resources, ingenuity – or even faith. It was "while we were still sinners", the Apostle Paul reminds us, that Christ died for us (Romans 5:8). In other words, the initiative in acting for our salvation rested wholly with God. In his letter to the Ephesians, Paul reminds us that we, by nature, were "dead", spiritually: not asleep, not unconscious, but dead. To be dead means to be incapable of rousing ourselves. "But God, being rich in mercy, because of the great love with which he loved us, even when we were dead in our trespasses, made us alive together with Christ" (Ephesians 2:4,5).

We have a word to describe that sovereign initiative of God in our lives, and it is arguably the most beautiful word in the Bible: grace. In fact, Paul adds it to the end of the verse just quoted: "by grace you have been saved".

Very few Christians will have any difficulty embracing the concept of grace when it comes to our eternal salvation. The very act of having come to the cross of Christ in repentance and faith means we have reached the point where we have become conscious of our sinfulness before God and our need of his mercy. We rejoice in the good news that Jesus died for us, that our sins are forgiven, and that we have peace with God, through Jesus Christ. It is with the deepest joy and the most heartfelt gratitude that we echo the words of John Newton's famous hymn: "*Amazing grace, how sweet the sound – that saved a wretch like me!*"

However, there is a rather more subtle trap that Christians can fall into. It is that of living as though – once saved by the death of Jesus – we are then to go on serving the Lord throughout our lives with all the strength *we* can muster.

It's a very subtle temptation. Have you ever heard the saying, "God helps those who help themselves"? Initially it might sound plausible – even biblical: after all, it is clear from Scripture that Christianity is intended to be an active, not a passive, faith. The mistake comes when we are tempted to be active *in our own strength*.

In the West, our wealth of resources, technology and consumer-savvy marketing techniques can easily, almost unobtrusively, create within us the illusion that *we* can build the kingdom. But this sort of mentality can easily lead to outreach programmes that are designed merely to attract as many people as possible rather than to challenge people to come to Christ in genuine, conscious repentance and faith.

And so we come to the third way in which engaging with the reality of persecution around the world can be of great blessing to us: it challenges a Western, self-sufficient view of life by deepening our desire for God's *grace*.

As we make ourselves aware of the situations in which Christians around the world find themselves, we see God's grace at work. This serves both as an encouragement to us in our own walk with the Lord, but also as a prompt to pray that God will continue to provide his grace where it is needed.

Furthermore, during a time when there are precious few signs of real growth in the Western church, we might well ask if there are lessons we can learn from the persecuted church.

Depending on the Lord

The Apostle Paul sums up the godly balance of an active Christianity lived in God's strength when he writes to the Philippians: "Work out your own salvation with fear and trembling, for it is God who works in you, both to will and to work for his good pleasure" (Philippians: 2:12,13).

We need reminding that we never move away from, or

beyond, the grace found at the cross, in terms of faithful Christian living. The grace that first brought us to the cross in repentance and saving faith is the same grace that sustains us and works in us throughout our Christian lives.

And, almost by definition, it tends to be in our weakness – rather than in our competence – that we are reminded of this.

In the midst of opposition, persecution and suffering, Christians learn of the need to rely not on themselves, but on the Lord. Paul articulated and exemplified this in his second letter to the Corinthians. "For we do not want you to be ignorant, brothers, of the affliction we experienced in Asia. For we were so utterly burdened beyond our strength that we despaired of life itself. Indeed, we felt that we had received the sentence of death. But that was to make us rely not on ourselves but on God who raises the dead" (2 Corinthians 1:8,9).

An African archbishop once said to me that each experience of persecution tests one's theology. That makes sense, and rings true. And that testing begins at the point of our reliance upon, and trust in, the God we believe in and worship. The God we declare to be almighty and sovereign over all. The God we believe loves us – even when, for reasons we don't fully understand, we are allowed to suffer.

Paul's point was that, as he laboured for the gospel in Asia, his suffering for that gospel drove him back to the Lord. Or, to put it in the language of this chapter's title, it stirred in him a deeper desire for God's sustaining and strengthening grace.

In one sense it could be said that this principle holds true for all forms of suffering. As we face all manner of trials, be they physical, emotional, financial or whatever, we as Christians may find ourselves running to the Lord for the strength to carry on. However, persecution – suffering for no other reason than because one stands for Christ and the gospel – brings our trust in the Lord into particularly sharp focus.

To meet or hear of Christians around the world who have lived through the painful and draining experience of persecution is to be confronted with believers who have learnt deep, lasting lessons about trusting in the Lord in all situations - trusting in the Lord when the circumstances around you would tempt you to question the wisdom or value of trusting in that Lord.

It is to our benefit to 'allow' them, if I can put it like that, to share with us what they have learnt in and through their experiences of suffering. That was Paul's point in the paragraph we have just been considering. He begins by praising "the Father of mercies and God of all comfort, who comforts us in all our affliction, so that we may be able to comfort those who are in any affliction, with the comfort with which we ourselves are comforted by God" (2 Corinthians 1:3,4). It is, perhaps, sometimes tempting to think that engaging too much with persecution is likely to be depressing; that we would rather not have to think about Christians suffering for their faith. The testimony of Scripture is that, actually, it can be to our comfort and blessing to do so.

Many of the psalms, particularly those commentators consider 'laments', speak of situations where people learn to depend on the Lord in and through opposition and suffering. Psalm 31 is a fine example of this – not least because Jesus quotes from it at the end of his own experience of suffering on the cross (Luke 23:46, quoting Psalm 31:5).

David's prayers for deliverance in Psalm 31 were real

prayers, for we know from the biblical account of his life that some conspired against him and sought to kill him. The extent of the opposition he faced is evident in the strong descriptive language he uses (verses 9-13) and he admits that he reached the point of virtually giving up on believing the Lord would help him (verse 22). And yet, ultimately, he maintains his trust in the Lord and continues to express his dependence on him. Notice how the plea, "Be a rock of refuge for me, a strong fortress to save me" (verse 2), is rooted in what David believes to be true of God: "For you *are* [my emphasis] my rock and my fortress" (verse 3).

This dependence on the Lord has been fashioned in the fires of persecution and is expressed in the face of all David is suffering. He continues to trust in the Lord *despite* his suffering. This makes Jesus' use of this psalm, as he hung on the cross, wholly appropriate. Jesus was not protected (in the sense of being spared) from those who sought to kill him, but continued to express dependence on the Lord God, nonetheless. As the Apostle Peter summed it up: "When he was reviled, he did not revile in return; when he suffered, he did not threaten, but continued entrusting himself to him who judges justly" (1 Peter 2:23).

Psalm 31 ends with David exhorting and encouraging his readers to maintain their own trust in the Lord (verses 23,24). The person who has been through severe persecution becomes a blessing to other believers, as they share their experience and what they know of depending on the Lord, and on his grace.

I know of a Christian family from northwest China. The husband, a pastor, was in prison as a result of his gospel ministry. His wife testified to the difficulties and setbacks she faced – including being barred from visiting her husband in prison for two years. She spoke, movingly, of their ten-year-old son praying that God would bring his father home, and of how often she felt helpless and weak, and unable to keep going. And yet she also testified to the grace of God encouraging her, pointing particularly to the Apostle Paul's declaration: "Since we have been justified by faith, we have peace with God through our Lord Jesus Christ. Through him we have also obtained access by faith into this grace in which we stand, and we rejoice in hope of the glory of God" (Romans 5:1,2).

Notice what this sister in the faith was *not* saying. She was not suggesting that, because she is a Christian, life is a breeze, an effortless journey of unremitting happiness and triumph. She was not claiming, or (worse) pretending, that faith in the grace of God meant all the hardships she and her family were going through were like water off a duck's back. No. The struggles and the pain she felt were real. The frustrating weakness and helplessness were real. Yet, she knew God was sustaining her *through* that pain. Such a spiritually mature testimony, grounded in reality and in Scripture, encourages our faith.

It is worth mentioning at this point the story of Job. Most Christian writers addressing any aspect of suffering will, not surprisingly, refer at some point to the Book of Job. In one sense, Job is not strictly about persecution. True, we are given insight in the opening two chapters of Job into the satanic origin of his sufferings. But not all Satan's evil activity in the world should be labelled as persecution (although in Chapter 2 we named Satan's opposition to the gospel as a spiritual reason for persecution). Our focus here is what the story says about depending on the Lord of grace.

The bulk of the book is taken up with the counsel of Job's friends. Their attitude to Job's calamities is based on an unbending understanding of cause and effect: namely, that human suffering is a direct result of human sin. If Job is suffering, there is clearly some specific and significant sin in his life that he needs to repent of.

There is no suggestion that Job would deny the reality of human sin – but that's not the point. What he objects to is his friends' simplistic interpretation of suffering. And yet at the same time he struggles with what has happened to him. He even admits his desire to confront God for some sort of answer, declaring at one point: "But I would speak to the Almighty, and I desire to argue my case with God" (Job 13:3).

What really interests us here, however, is the book's conclusion. When Job's friends have had their say, the Lord, in his grace, speaks to Job. In doing so, though, he does not aim to satisfy Job's desire for an answer; he does not (as far as we can see) reveal to Job Satan's involvement, or explain why he, in his sovereignty, *allowed* Satan to bring about the series of calamities. In short, God does not see the need to justify himself to Job. Rather, the Lord presents his own glory and character (chapters 38-41). At first, Job is silenced (Job 40:3-5), and then moved to repent (Job 42:6). (The context makes it clear that he is repenting of the attitude he showed towards God *as a result of* his suffering – rather than repenting of a particular sin that *caused* his suffering.) Job needs to know the God in whom he can depend: the God who gives the necessary grace.

By the end of the story, we might say that although God has not given Job his answers, he has answered Job! In his meeting with the Lord, Job knows he can depend on him.

In travelling around the world and meeting with Christians living at the sharp end of opposition to the gospel, I have been struck by how often they express this sort of godly dependence. "I just take everything to the Lord," or, "My God will do everything for me." These are not empty phrases, recited to maintain some respectable veneer of orthodox faith. No, they express a deep dependence on God, fashioned and matured in the fire of opposition and suffering for Christ.

Persevering with the Lord

Closely allied to the need to depend on the Lord comes the call to persevere with the Lord throughout our Christian lives. This is, in many ways, the dominant theme we observe when reflecting on what Scripture says about responding to persecution when we experience it ourselves. In the context of the mission they were to carry out in his name, Jesus told his disciples, "You will be hated by all for my name's sake. But the one who endures to the end will be saved" (Matthew 10:22). This call to endure is even more striking when one realises Jesus has just spoken about experiencing opposition even from our nearest and dearest (Matthew 10:21).

It is often said that we live in an age when nobody *sticks* at things. Ours is a restless culture. On the one hand, people quickly become bored and want fresh stimulus and excitement. At the same time, the trials, difficulties and conflicts of life cause many to bid an all too hasty retreat and to seek a fresh start somewhere else.

In the face of prevailing attitudes around us, Christians are called to persevere in their walk with the Lord. The passage from which we have just quoted in Matthew's Gospel (which we also referred to in Chapter 2) is a reminder of that. In sending his disciples out on a mission, Jesus places great emphasis on the opposition they will encounter from the world. But far from playing this down, or soft-peddling it, Jesus uses this reality to emphasise the need to persevere. "So everyone who acknowledges me before men, I also will acknowledge before my Father who is in heaven, but whoever denies me before men, I also will deny before my Father who is in heaven" (Matthew 10:32,33).

Where do we find the resources to do this: to persevere faithfully in the face of opposition, threats, intimidation or violence? Not from within ourselves. In fact, we are warned in the Scriptures that persecution can potentially be a real danger to faith. In Jesus' Parable of the Sower, the seed that fell on rocky ground is later described by Jesus as representing the kind of follower who "has no root in himself, but endures for a while, and when tribulation or persecution arises on account of the word, immediately he falls away" (Matthew 13:21).

No, humanly speaking, persecution endangers faith. Humanly speaking, persecution is more likely to lead us to hide, to be silent, or, worse, even to deny our faith – if all we had were our own resources and strength. But the resources we need are found in the Lord himself. Persecution teaches this. It exposes the inadequacy of a 'self-sufficient' attitude to life and deepens our desire for God's sustaining grace. Once again, the dominant overall theme of our book comes to the surface. For we Christians in the West, engaging with the issue of persecution is not just about praying for our persecuted brothers and sisters and providing materially for their needs (although such acts are fundamentally part of our responsibility); it is also about walking with them and learning with them the lessons of discipleship.

The clarion call to persevere in the face of opposition is

so significant that a whole New Testament book is devoted to the theme: the majestic letter to the Hebrews.

Think of Hebrews and you think of some of its distinctive contributions to New Testament faith and teaching: Jesus as God's full and final revelation to mankind; the superiority of Christ over every aspect of the Old Covenant that he came to fulfil; and, of course, his role as our great high priest, who not only sacrificed himself once for all (in contrast to the repeated sacrifices of animals by the Jewish priest) but who also now lives to plead on our behalf at the right hand of God.

And yet these important themes and subjects all serve the greater purpose of the letter: to encourage persecuted Christians to persevere in their faith.

The letter was written, it seems, to Jewish Christians who were struggling in the face of opposition, and who were showing signs of drifting away from Christ and returning to the comparatively safer haven of Judaism. The way in which Christ fulfils, and is superior to, all aspects of the Old Covenant served to emphasise the folly of succumbing to the temptation to do so.

The various arguments and themes build towards the final chapters of the letter, in which the readers are called to persevere in faithfully following Christ. Having cited, as examples, a great list of Old Covenant believers in Hebrews 11 (some of whom "conquered kingdoms" and "stopped the mouths of lions", while others, by contrast, "were tortured", "suffered mocking" and "imprisonment" and were killed), the writer urges them to "run with endurance" the race of faith. That means continuing to look to Jesus, the Jesus who "for the joy that was set before him endured the cross, despising the shame, and is seated at the right hand of the throne of God" (Hebrews 12:2). The appeal of the letter may be summed up in the next verse: "Consider him who endured from sinners such hostility against himself, so that you may not grow weary or fainthearted" (Hebrews 12:3).

To look to Jesus must mean to continue in the Christian faith, but it also meant, in this context, to trust in him to strengthen them and to enable them to respond in the way the writer is urging. As he reminded them earlier in the letter: "Since we have a great high priest who has passed through the heavens, Jesus, the Son of God, let us hold fast our confession. For we do not have a high priest who is unable to sympathise with our weaknesses, but one who in every respect has been tempted as we are, yet without sin. Let us then with confidence draw near to the throne of grace, that we may receive mercy and find grace to help in time of need" (Hebrews 4:14-16).

Grace to help in time of need. This is something every Christian needs to understand and hold on to. Our God is a God we can call upon to give the necessary grace where and when it is needed. If perseverance is the fundamental response to persecution, then engaging with the realities of persecution will inevitably deepen our desire for grace, both for ourselves and for our fellow Christians around the world.

Testifying to the Lord

Throughout the history of the church, Christians have reflected on, and wrestled with, the relationship between persecution and the spread of the gospel.

Early in the Book of Acts, we read, following the stoning of Stephen: "And there arose on that day a great persecution against the church in Jerusalem, and they were all scattered throughout the regions of Judea and

Samaria..." (Acts 8:1). Intriguingly, a couple of verses later, Luke comments: "Now those who were scattered went about preaching the word" (Acts 8:4). The inference is that the persecution that broke out in Jerusalem only served to spread the gospel further afield!

In the following chapter, the link between persecution and the spread of the gospel is further suggested in the commissioning of the recently converted Paul (or Saul, as he was still referred to at that point). Speaking to Ananias, who was to go and minister to Saul, the Lord says: "Go, for he is a chosen instrument of mine to carry my name before the Gentiles and kings and the children of Israel. For I will show him how much he must suffer for the sake of my name" (Acts 9:15,16).

One might add that the whole flow of the Book of Acts continues to make this point. At times persecution leads to people coming to faith (for example, in Acts 16 where the conversion of the Philippian jailer could be said to be a direct result of Paul's night in prison); at other times it leads to the gospel being proclaimed in new places.

When Paul writes to the Christians in Philippi from his prison cell in Rome, he is able to declare: "I want you to know, brothers, that what has happened to me has really served to advance the gospel, so that it has become known throughout the whole imperial guard and to all the rest that my imprisonment is for Christ. And most of the brothers, having become confident in the Lord by my imprisonment, are much more bold to speak the word without fear" (Philippians 1:12-14).

That final sentence is fascinating, to say the least. One might have assumed that Paul's imprisonment would have led the Christians in Rome to become more circumspect about sharing the gospel, but it appears from what Paul writes that the opposite was the case. They somehow drew courage and inspiration from Paul's experience and began testifying with greater boldness.

Moving beyond Scripture into the pages of church history we could chart other times over the past 2,000 years when severe persecution has led to the spread of the gospel and the consequential growth of the church. In this context, it is popular to quote Tertullian, a famous, second-century theologian from North Africa, who wrote: "The blood of the martyrs is the seed of the church." There can be no denying that God can – and often has – used the persecution of his people to further his kingdom. This should not surprise us, knowing we have a God who is sovereign over all things, and who works all things according to the counsel of his will.

However, we must never assume that there is an automatic, inextricable link between persecution and the growth of the church. We are not talking about some impersonal equation: we are talking about people, and people's lives. Church history also records occasions when persecution has all but snuffed out the church, or has divided and weakened the church, thus stunting its growth.

Yes, God can, and has, used persecution to further his kingdom – but that, of course, is the point: it is *God* who can do this. We can rely on him to work in and through all things for his eternal purposes, and faith does so. But that is not the same as *presuming* upon him to act in a particular way in and through a particular set of circumstances. Where the church has not only survived, but has grown in and through an experience of persecution, it is only ever through the sovereign grace of God. Persecution deepens our desire for that grace.

That desire for grace will, in the life of the Christian, express itself in prayer. Writing at the end of his second letter to the Thessalonian Christians, Paul says: "Finally, brothers, pray for us, that the word of the Lord may speed ahead and be honoured, as happened among you" (2 Thessalonians 3:1). Paul is asking the Thessalonian Christians to pray that, by God's grace, the gospel will continue to spread. 'Pray that the gospel will *run*' is the sense of the word Paul uses: run far and wide, and be glorified as lives are changed. Here is a fine, straightforward example of requesting prayer for the effectiveness of Christian gospel witness and mission.

But in the next breath he adds: "And [pray that] we may be delivered from wicked and evil men. For not all have faith" (2 Thessalonians 3:2). In Chapter 2, we saw that the sinful human nature naturally rejects the light of the gospel of Christ. Everywhere the gospel goes, it is opposed. Only by God's grace does anyone receive it. The Thessalonian Christians were aware of this. In his first letter to them, Paul thanks God that they came to faith (1 Thessalonians 1:2-10). If it is only by God's grace that anyone receives the gospel then, naturally, we should thank God when someone does so! He then goes on to remind the Thessalonians how, having received the word of God, they immediately experienced opposition themselves (1 Thessalonians 2:13,14)!

Paul's twin prayer request (for the gospel to spread and for its ministers to be protected) towards the end of his second letter confirms what we have argued earlier in this book – and our theme here. When we see and hear of persecution, we should not be surprised – but neither should we be inactive. Its existence deepens our desire to seek God's grace in prayer.

Forgiving in the Lord

Every Christian is familiar with the Lord's Prayer, and

many Christians will belong to church families that regularly pray it together in corporate worship. Down the years, its 57 words (in the original Greek of Matthew's Gospel) have spawned countless books, booklets and articles, exploring the meaning of each of the petitions and encouraging us to see the prayer as a framework on which to build and shape all our prayers.

It is interesting to consider, then, that one of the best-known parts of Christian Scripture (and certainly the best-known prayer in Christian history) should also contain one of the hardest things – emotionally – that we will ever be asked to do as we seek to walk this life in obedience to the Lord Jesus Christ.

"Forgive us our sins, as we forgive those who sin against us." The phrase trips easily off the tongue, because we know it so well. But what is it actually saying?

Matthew's version (Matthew 6:9-13) actually uses the word "debts" although Luke, in his slightly abbreviated version of the prayer (Luke 11:2-4), uses "sins". In practice there is unlikely to be any difference between the two accounts, as Matthew may have been employing a literal rendering of an Aramaic word used by Jesus, which was often used to mean 'sin'. This possibility is reinforced by the fact that in the following verse Jesus emphasises this particular petition, adding: "For if you forgive others their trespasses, your heavenly Father will also forgive you" (Matthew 6:14).

Many commentators and preachers are quick to point out that, despite what might appear to be the case on the surface, Jesus cannot be implying that we can *earn*, or *deserve,* God's forgiveness by the act of forgiving others. This would, after all, render Jesus' work on the cross redundant.

It *is* important, however, to recognise that the New Testament repeatedly emphasises the importance of saving faith being worked out in our lives. At times this is stressed by the use of phrases that, taken in isolation, might appear to suggest that we can earn grace and favour from God. One example of this is Paul's words to the Roman Christians, declaring that we are "fellow heirs with Christ, *provided* we suffer with him in order that we may also be glorified with him" (Romans 8:17). In a letter that has spelled out so comprehensively the gospel of justification by grace through faith, it would be incongruous, to say the least, if Paul were now muddying the waters by suggesting we can *earn* an eternal inheritance merely by being willing to suffer for the name of Christ. No, he isn't – but grace, once received, needs to be *seen*.

The Sermon on the Mount (of which the Lord's Prayer is part) is addressed to those who are already 'disciples' of Jesus (Matthew 5:1,2). As disciples we ought to be conscious of our need for God's forgiveness – and at least part of the evidence for that will be seen (or ought to be seen) in our willingness to forgive others. To ask from God what we refuse to offer others would appear insulting and presumptuous. This interpretation of Jesus' words in the Lord's Prayer is reinforced later in Matthew's Gospel. "Then Peter came up and said to him, 'Lord, how often will my brother sin against me, and I forgive him? As many as seven times?' Jesus said to him, 'I do not say to you seven times, but seventy-seven times'" – an answer which surely is implying we ought not to put limits on our willingness to forgive (Matthew 18:21,22). Jesus then goes on to tell the Parable of the Unforgiving Servant (Matthew 18:23-35) which exposes the hypocrisy of seeking forgiveness while being unwilling to forgive others. Moreover, in that parable the unforgiving servant is forgiven for a far greater debt than the debt he was *unwilling* to forgive another. This, surely, is the crux of the matter for us as Christians. To appreciate the enormity of our sin in the face of a holy God is to see others' offences and trespasses against us in their proper proportion.

It is, however, one thing to tease out the meaning of Jesus' words in the Lord's Prayer – and quite another to put that into practice. Weak, frail, imperfect – and sinful – we remain, even if redeemed by Christ's blood and inhabited by Christ's Spirit. How easy it is to desire and pray for God's forgiveness, while at the same time harbouring resentment and holding things against other people.

Yes, it is emotionally difficult. But, as we noted earlier in the chapter, we are not to live this life in our own strength, but in the strength that God provides.

Here, I believe, is one of the most profoundly powerful lessons we can learn from those who have lived through the trauma of severe persecution: knowing the grace of God that enables us to forgive.

I first encountered this when I heard the story of a Nigerian pastor whose Christian community had been attacked by a group of Islamic militants, armed with guns and machetes. Many members of his church were slaughtered in the attack – including his wife and daughter. He spoke, movingly, of how Jesus Christ helped him to forgive.

I later had the privilege of meeting a housewife, from the same country, who had seen three teenage family members shot dead in her home by another group of armed militants. It was a horrific ordeal. And yet, she, too, was able to say she forgave those who had attacked her home and family. When we Christians in the West hear such stories, it is tempting to react in two ways. First, to say, "I don't think I could respond like that if such an awful thing happened to me." The second is to then gaze upon those whose stories we have heard with something of a reverent awe. Both reactions are understandable, but what we should do, of course, is to praise God for his sustaining grace. Christians who persevere in faithfulness and who demonstrate a Christ-like attitude in and through such trials are neither super-human nor unfeeling. When they are able to show forgiveness, in the face of such horror and suffering, it is to the glory of God - the God who can provide grace where and when it is needed. Their testimonies are a reminder that God does, indeed, provide grace where it is needed.

For those of us living in more comfortable circumstances, the witness of faithful, persecuted Christians is both a challenge and an encouragement. It challenges our faith and the priority we attach to seeking the grace of God in prayer, reminding us that we are not called to live this life in our own strength, but in the strength that God provides. At the same time, the witness of faithful, persecuted Christians encourages us, for in the lives of such people we see flesh-and-blood evidence of that grace at work in the world today: grace that is available to us, too, when we most need it, as we seek to live faithfully for the Lord.

Your response

1. Read Psalm 31. What does David learn about God's grace in and through affliction and persecution?

2. Where in your own life have you been most aware of the grace of God?

3. How do you react when you hear of persecuted Christians forgiving their attackers? In what way is their testimony a challenge or an encouragement to you?

Chapter 4

Broadening our experience of church

I t was John Wesley who said, "There is no such thing as a solitary Christian."

The Christian faith is, of course, a *personal* faith. Unlike other world religions, Christianity, properly understood, is not simply a culture you can be born into. The Christian gospel is a message to be heard, understood and responded to. It declares that, in the person of Jesus Christ, God has acted at a point in history in a unique way, to reconcile mankind to himself. The Apostle Peter summed this up when he told a group of Jewish religious leaders: "There is salvation in no one else, for there is no other name under heaven given among men by which we must be saved" (Acts 4:12).

Furthermore, that gospel requires a response: one in which we acknowledge before God our guilt, our need of his mercy and our belief that Jesus Christ has made that mercy possible by dying in our place on the cross. Trusting in his death as our saviour, we now seek to follow him as our Lord. The Apostle Paul described how his gospel ministry called people to this response, when he told church elders in Ephesus that he had been "testifying both to Jews and to Greeks [in other words, to everyone, regardless of their religious background] of repentance toward God and of faith in our Lord Jesus Christ" (Acts 20:21).

All of this emphasises the personal nature of Christian faith.

However, the Scriptures make it clear that this personal, life-changing decision does not leave me as an isolated, individual follower of Jesus. To become a follower of Jesus is to become part of the *people*, or family, of God. The New Testament uses a variety of images to describe this family, many of them drawn from the Old Testament, indicating how the church of Jesus Christ is the fulfilment of Old Testament Israel as God's people. A classic example of this is found in the Apostle Peter's first letter. He writes, piling up images culled from the Old Testament: "As you come to him [Christ], a living stone rejected by men but in the sight of God chosen and precious, you yourselves like living stones are being built up as a spiritual house, to be a holy priesthood, to offer spiritual sacrifices to God... you are a chosen race, a royal priesthood, a holy nation, a people for his own possession... Once you were not a people, but now you are God's people; once you had not received mercy, but now you have received mercy" (1 Peter 2:4,5, 9,10). United to Christ by faith, Christians are now the true temple, where God is present (see also Ephesians 2:19-22).

To be incorporated into the church of Jesus Christ brings both blessing and responsibility. We have the blessing of Christian fellowship, that unique, supernatural bond of people from all backgrounds who have been united by faith in Christ to worship, witness and walk in faith together. But this also brings responsibility: a willingness to serve Christ our Lord in and through the life of his church.

For fairly obvious and practical reasons, that commitment and service will begin in the *local* Christian community to which we belong. This is what most of us tend to mean, first of all, when we talk about 'church' (hence the common question Christians ask one another: "So which church do you go to, then?"). It is in this local gathering of believers that we offer our gifts, share in Christian service and seek to worship and witness week by week.

Ultimately, however, there is one church, one people of God, one 'body of Christ', for Christ is the representative 'head' of that body (Ephesians 1:22,23). For this reason our commitment and service should never end with the local congregation we belong to, even if it begins there. A desire to serve Christ and a zeal for his gospel have always inspired Christians to look beyond their own parochial context, and to engage prayerfully and practically with what is happening elsewhere in God's world.

And so we come to the fourth way in which engaging seriously with issues of persecution can be a blessing to us. It challenges a purely individualistic view of the kingdom, by broadening our experience of church.

Unity of the body

The idea of the church as a 'body', more specifically as the body of Christ, is a concept we associate with the teaching of the Apostle Paul. It is a very powerful image, and a challenging one, particularly in our individualistic Western world. Paul uses it to teach that, although we are all different, we belong together *in Christ* (1 Corinthians 12:14-31). We should not be made to feel excluded, nor should we make others feel excluded, if we share the same saving faith in the Lord.

This 'body' image, with Christ as our head, emphasises the unity, or oneness, that exists in the church of Jesus Christ. Paul writes to the Corinthians: "For just as

71

the body is one and has many members, and all the members of the body, though many, are one body, so it is with Christ. For in one Spirit we were all baptised into one body – Jews or Greeks, slaves or free – and all were made to drink of one Spirit" (1 Corinthians 12:12,13).

Human nature being what it is (even human nature that has been renewed by the grace of God), that unity is not always easily maintained, and so the 'body' image is not only stated as a doctrine, it is also used by Paul as an exhortation. To the Ephesians he writes: "I… urge you to walk in a manner worthy of the calling to which you have been called, with all humility and gentleness, with patience, bearing with one another in love, eager to maintain the unity of the Spirit in the bond of peace. There is one body and one Spirit – just as you were called to the one hope that belongs to your call…" (Ephesians 4:1-4).

Engaging with those who are suffering severe persecution for their faith in Christ is one very clear way – both as individuals and as local church communities – that we can express, and benefit from experiencing, that oneness or unity. To visit and meet Christians in other parts of the world who have known significant persecution for their faith in Christ can be humbling – but also rewarding. The spiritual bond we have in Christ is something we don't always appreciate within our own church communities, but it is amplified in the cauldron of suffering for the faith. Those who have harrowing stories of persecution to tell take great encouragement from the fact that the church in the West knows about their plight – and cares. We can't all physically 'go', but we can find and develop ways of learning about, identifying with, and supporting our suffering brothers and sisters in Christ. Very often this will be by connecting with and supporting mission agencies that provide care for persecuted Christians around the world.

In his extended treatment of the 'body' image in 1 Corinthians, Paul declares, "If one member suffers, all suffer together..." (1 Corinthians 12:26). This is true of the human body, of course. If I stub my toe, it is with my mouth that I cry out in pain; if I graze my knee, it is with my hands that I apply ointment and a plaster.

This principle of expressing our oneness in Christ in the midst of suffering or trouble is something many of us will be well aware of and will have experienced within our own local church fellowships. If somebody in the congregation is in hospital, others will pay a visit or provide some practical assistance; and we would probably pray for that person when we gathered as a church on a Sunday, or at a midweek prayer meeting.

To connect with Christians around the world who are suffering for the gospel is, however, to take that expression of oneness and unity to a deeper level, and one that can be enriching for our faith as we see, experience and express what it means to be a follower of Jesus Christ and to be part of his body that suffers the hatred of the world and its rejection of the Lord.

At various points in the New Testament, we see the Apostle Paul promoting the collection he took among Gentile churches to support the impoverished Jewish-Christian church in Judaea. I believe that for Paul the importance of this collection lay not just in issues of fairness and justice (the wealthier caring for the poorer), but in the theological oneness it expressed: the unity of the body of Christ. We have the opportunity to express that same oneness today as we identify with, and provide for, those who are suffering for the same faith we profess.

In the previous chapter we noted that the letter to the

Hebrews was written to encourage and to exhort Christians to persevere in their faith in the midst of opposition (Hebrews 13:22). Interestingly, at the beginning of the final chapter, the writer urges his readers to "Remember those who are in prison, as though in prison with them, and those who are mistreated..." (Hebrews 13:3).

The context would suggest that the people his readers should remember are (a) fellow Christians, and (b) Christians who are in prison, or being mistreated, for their faith; in other words, *because* they are Christians. The writer's concern for his readers' own faltering faith does not stop him urging them to be concerned for others, in fact, quite the opposite. It is not going too far, I believe, to suggest that if caring for fellow Christians is part of our responsibility as members of the body, getting on and doing so actually becomes one means of reinvigorating our own faith! Earlier the writer reminded them of the zeal they had displayed when they themselves first became Christians: "But recall the former days when, after you were enlightened, you endured a hard struggle with sufferings, sometimes being publicly exposed to reproach and affliction, and sometimes being partners with those so treated. For you had compassion on those in prison..." (Hebrews 10:32-34). In other words, what he is urging them to do (in Hebrews 13:3) is something he knows they have managed to do in the past.

To engage with, and to demonstrate a real care for, our fellow Christians who are suffering persecution is actually an important aspect of our discipleship. It is to the benefit of our own spiritual health – both individually and as a local congregation. Moreover, the New Testament's teaching on the unity and bond we have within the body of Christ marks it out as a fundamental responsibility that we should not shirk.

Learning as a body

It could be argued that in one sense the previous chapter constitutes the theological centre, or hub, of the entire book, for everything in life – and certainly in Christian living – flows from the sovereign grace of God.

That being so, we might say that we have arrived here at something of a practical centre, or focus. Throughout this book, we have been suggesting that engaging meaningfully with the persecution of Christians around the world can be a real blessing to us. That blessing comes in the context of the relationships we have within the body of Christ.

Christian faith, as we said at the beginning of this chapter, is personal – but the Christian life is then lived out in the context of being part of God's family. Discipleship is, or ought to be, the shared experience of the redeemed people of God – and that includes our attitude to persecution.

We see this illustrated powerfully in Romans 12. Paul begins the chapter: "I appeal to you therefore, brothers, by the mercies of God..." (Romans 12:1). As many a Bible teacher has pointed out, whenever we read a word like "therefore" in the Scriptures, it forces us to look backwards in the text, for the writer is making a link with something he has written earlier. "Because what I have just written is true, *therefore*, in the light of that, I am now saying..."

What is Paul referring back to in this instance at the beginning of Romans 12? Probably everything he has written in the letter up to this point! In his letter to the Romans, Paul, inspired by God, sets out the most comprehensive, systematic, logical explanation of the gospel and its benefits that we find in the New Testament. He spends two-and-a-half chapters emphasising the fact that every human being without exception – Gentile and Jew alike – stands naturally condemned before God as a sinful rebel. This is followed by the most sublime definition of what God has done to reconcile us to himself through the sacrifice of his Son, and how we are to receive the benefits of that work: by faith alone. In chapters 5-8, Paul then moves on to the assurance that this gospel gives us, building to a mini-climax (see Romans 8:37-39) in which he rejoices in the certainty that the Christian has in Christ. However, no analysis of the gospel would be complete without reflection on how it fits in with the earthly promises made by God to his Old Testament people – which is what Paul goes on to do in chapters 9-11.

His analysis complete, Paul's response to this glorious gospel is one of overriding praise and wonder: "Oh, the depth of the riches and wisdom and knowledge of God...! For from him and through him and to him are all things. To him be glory for ever. Amen" (Romans 11:33, 36).

Amen, indeed. Praise and thanksgiving will ever be the appropriate response of the Christian to what God has done for us in Christ. But then comes the application. It is in the light of this gospel, set before us so thoroughly, that Paul now writes: "I appeal to you *therefore*, brothers, by the mercies of God, to present your bodies as a living sacrifice, holy and acceptable to God, which is your spiritual worship" (Romans 12:1).

Chapter 12 marks a turning point, or hinge, in the letter. In the light of the overwhelming mercy and grace God has shown us, we are to give the whole of our lives to him. This wholehearted response, embracing every aspect of our lives, is the true meaning of 'worship'.

The rest of the letter is taken up with some examples of what this will mean in practice. Some, from chapter 13 onwards, are dealt with in detail, but here in chapter 12 Paul begins by reeling off a breathless list of illustrations with machine-gun rapidity (Romans 12:3-21)!

If we wanted a concept that holds all of these examples together, it would be that of *relationship*. Discipleship is the shared experience of the redeemed people of God, so Paul first encourages us to have a proper, biblical view of ourselves as part of the body of Christ (Romans 12:3-8), and then to make 'love' the abiding characteristic of our relationships – both in that body and in the world around us (Romans 12:9-21).

Significantly, as far as our relationship with the world is concerned, it is the latter's hostility that is foremost in the Apostle Paul's mind here (Romans 12:12 and then verses 14-21). In that context, 'worshipping' God will mean being patient in tribulation (verse 12); it will mean blessing those who persecute us (verse 14); it will mean having no thought for revenge (verses 17 and 19), but rather maintaining a loving attitude to those who might persecute us (verses 18 and 20,21).

Notice how, woven into these verses, Paul makes mention of the importance of caring for our fellow Christians when they suffer: "Be constant in prayer. Contribute to the needs of the saints" (Romans 12:12,13); "weep with those who weep" (verse 15); "do not be haughty, but associate with the lowly" (verse 16). The hostility of the world, the way we react to it, and the way we care for our needy and suffering fellow Christians are bound tightly together in these verses as illustrations of giving ourselves wholly to the Lord, in response to the mercy he has shown us.

Furthermore, as we have already noted, these verses in

the latter part of the chapter are preceded by Paul's first example of 'worship', which is to see ourselves as part of the body of Christ, with gifts and resources which are to be used for the good of that body (Romans 12:3-8). Discipleship is the shared experience of the people of God. It is, therefore, as one body that we respond to, and learn from, the experience of persecution.

This is important, pastorally and practically. We have already noted, earlier in this book, that Christians in the West today have not, on the whole, experienced first-hand the more severe forms of persecution endured by our brothers and sisters in Christ in other parts of the world. Does this mean we are missing out on a vital aspect of our discipleship? And if so, is it right to yearn for similar experiences of persecution ourselves?

Throughout my Christian life, I have, from time to time, come across Christians who have expressed a sentiment along those lines. "I think we could do with a dose of persecution in this country..." More often than not, this view has been prompted by reflection on either the lack of evangelistic zeal in churches in the West, or their doctrinal laxity. The obvious implication is that a dose of persecution would shake us up a bit.

One can have some sympathy with that view (or, at least, with the frustration behind it) but, on the whole, it is inappropriate. Scripture does not encourage us to desire, still less to seek, persecution. To look no further than the life of the Apostle Paul, we see situations where, in fact, he does the opposite. At Damascus he was lowered down the city wall in a basket to avoid Jews who were trying to kill him (Acts 9:23-25); on his first missionary journey, he and Barnabas fled from Iconium when they learned that opponents were after them (Acts 14:5,6); later, he invoked his rights as a Roman citizen to avoid being whipped (Acts 22:22-29).

None of these examples ever justify our denying our faith to avoid suffering, but they do provide a valuable biblical check when it comes to reflecting on the place of persecution in the Christian life and our attitude to it. At the end of the day, persecution is never experienced uniformly and constantly – even in countries where the persecution of Christians is considered severe. One congregation may be attacked, another not. One pastor may be martyred, while many others are not. That fact alone is supportive of the point being made here: that we are to learn from persecution not by zealously and even recklessly seeking a similar experience of it for ourselves. Rather, we experience it *as the body of Christ*. For us in the West, at this point in history, that will mean engaging meaningfully with what is happening elsewhere in our world, identifying with Christians who are in the throes of severe suffering, seeking to support and encourage them, and pray for them – but also, together, as one body, allowing biblical truth to interpret what is being experienced, in order to sharpen our faith, and to fortify us in the service of Christ and his gospel.

Love for all the body

As we have just seen, a wholehearted response to the gospel of Christ will include relationships that are characterised by love. "Love one another with brotherly affection," writes Paul (Romans 12:10). In similar fashion, the night before he was crucified, Jesus said to his disciples: "Love one another; just as I have loved you, you also are to love one another. By this all people will know that you are my disciples, if you have love for one another" (John 13:34,35)

In this chapter, we have been arguing that engaging

with persecution challenges an individualistic view of the kingdom by broadening our experience of the church. A fundamental aspect of that experience of church is a demonstration of the love Jesus and the Apostle both spoke of: a love that is practical; a love that cares; a love that then becomes a powerful witness to the world of the reality of Jesus and of the difference he makes.

One extended illustration of that care (in the context of persecution) comes in the Apostle Paul's first letter to the Thessalonians. Paul's ministry in Thessalonica, during his second missionary journey, is recorded in Acts 17. Paul spent some time at the synagogue, reasoning with the Jews from the Scriptures (Acts 17:2,3) before eventually being forced to leave, after Jewish opposition to the gospel had led to a major city-wide disturbance (Acts 17:5-10).

What is clear from 1 Thessalonians is that a new church of believers had been formed at that time and that it wasn't long before these new Christians began to experience local opposition themselves (1 Thessalonians 2:14; also 1 Thessalonians 1:6,7). This should not have surprised them, for Paul had evidently taught them to expect this: "For when we were with you, we kept telling you beforehand that we were to suffer affliction, just as it has come to pass, and just as you know" (1 Thessalonians 3:4). We don't know exactly how long he had spent in the city, but in nurturing this fledgling congregation, Paul had evidently and quickly found time to teach them about opposition to the gospel. As far as Paul was concerned, this, it seems, was part of basic Christian teaching. If you or I were tasked with writing a nurture course to disciple new Christians in our church, would we instinctively include teaching on the hostility people might, or should expect, to face, having come to faith?

What we see in this first letter to the Thessalonians is all very much in line with what we said about the gospel and human nature in Chapter 2. But what really interests us at this point is Paul's concern for this young church. He had wanted to go and see them, but circumstances had hindered him, circumstances Paul attributes to the work of Satan (1 Thessalonians 2:17,18). Finally, when he could "bear it no longer", he sent his friend and co-worker Timothy to "establish and exhort" them (1 Thessalonians 3:1,2). Why? Because Paul evidently saw persecution as a real danger to the faith of these Thessalonians (1 Thessalonians 3:3, 5). He was concerned that they might fall away from faith in Christ as a result of the suffering they were experiencing.

Such is the pastoral heart of the Apostle. Do we Christians in the West have anything approaching this sort of pastoral heart for our persecuted brothers and sisters around the world today? Are we concerned for the possible impact of violent persecution, oppression and imprisonment on young Christian faith? What about the effect that the imprisonment and perhaps the torture of a pastor might have on the faith of his children? Is it our earnest desire to see Christians "established and exhorted" in the face of opposition to the gospel? Is it our genuine prayer that the faith of Christians will be deepened, rather than destroyed, as they experience first-hand the world's rejection of Jesus?

Paul is, of course, writing to these Thessalonians after Timothy had returned from his brief mission of discovery and encouragement – and Timothy had evidently come back with good news. Note the real sense of exuberant joy in Paul: "But now that Timothy has come to us from you, and has brought us the good news of your faith and love and reported that you always remember us kindly and long to see us, as we long to see you – for this reason, brothers, in all our distress and affliction we have been comforted about you through your faith. For now we live, if you are standing fast in the Lord" (1 Thessalonians 3:6-8).

Isn't that wonderful? To know that these young Thessalonian Christians were persevering in their faith – in the face of opposition – brought Paul deep joy. But not only that, it also encouraged *him* in the midst of *his* afflictions (1 Thessalonians 3:7). We might say Paul experienced the blessing that comes from engaging with, and caring for, Christians suffering for their faith.

Towards the end of his life, Paul would find himself on the receiving end of this kind of loving, pastoral Christian care.

Paul's second letter to Timothy is almost certainly the last letter of the Apostle we have in the New Testament. He is once again in prison, awaiting a trial that he believes will go against him (2 Timothy 4:6,7). Martyrdom, it seems, is his destiny in the very near future. For Paul, this marks something of a transitional moment: the passing on of leadership from an Apostle to the next generation. Paul writes to Timothy, a man he has known for a number of years, and who has served with him in gospel ministry.

The whole letter resonates with the importance of maintaining, guarding, teaching and continuing to proclaim the one true, Apostolic gospel: "Follow the pattern of sound words that you have heard from me" (2 Timothy 1:13). "What you have heard from me... entrust to faithful men who will be able to teach it to others also" (2 Timothy 2:2). "Present yourself to God as one approved... rightly handling the word of truth" (2 Timothy 2:15). "Preach the word; be ready in season and out of season; reprove, rebuke, and exhort" (2 Timothy 4:2).

Closely bound up with these exhortations is the recognition that the gospel will provoke opposition, both from within the church (heresy) and from without (persecution). Timothy would have been aware of this, of course, from the time he had spent with Paul, but it was good for him to be reminded. At the beginning of the letter, Paul encourages him not to be ashamed of the gospel, or of Paul, languishing in prison, but to "share in suffering" for the gospel (2 Timothy 1:8). This 'sharing' would, presumably, involve the possibility of direct suffering by Timothy himself, but perhaps also the 'indirect suffering' of identifying with those who suffered, as Paul was suffering.

In this regard, Paul cites the example of Onesiphorus. Not a particularly well-known name among all the characters we meet in the New Testament, but one for whom Paul was certainly thankful. "May the Lord grant mercy to the household of Onesiphorus, for he often refreshed me and was not ashamed of my chains, but when he arrived in Rome he searched for me earnestly and found me" (2 Timothy 1:16,17).

Onesiphorus means 'one who brings benefit to another', and he certainly lived up to his name! Visiting someone like Paul in prison could have been a risky business, as he would inevitably have been identifying himself with all that Paul stood for – and yet he took the trouble to go and find him. And in doing so, he "refreshed" the Apostle. What an epitaph!

Arguably, Onesiphorus was simply living out the teaching of Jesus. In his parable of the sheep and the goats (Matthew 25:31-46), Jesus describes those who will be blessed by God on the day of judgement in this way: "I was hungry and you gave me food, I was thirsty and you gave me drink, I was a stranger and you welcomed me, I was naked and you clothed me, I was sick and you visited me, I was in prison and you came to me" (Matthew 25:35,36). Those described in this way express surprise, asking when it was that they had treated Jesus in this laudable way. His reply is: "Truly, I say to you, as you did it to one of the least of these my *brothers*, you did it to me" (Matthew 25:40).

I agree with those commentators who give the word "brothers" a specific and narrow meaning and significance here. In Matthew's Gospel, "brothers" only ever refers either to the members of Jesus' extended earthly family or – more relevantly for us in this instance – to his followers. The latter use of the word is, of course, carried on into the rest of the New Testament where it becomes a common way of addressing fellow Christians. In other words, it would seem that Jesus is describing the way Christians should treat their fellow Christians.

Some people have argued that restricting the meaning of "brothers" in this passage to refer to our fellow Christians places unnecessary limits on the extent of practical, Christian love, to the point of debasing it. But that is to miss Jesus' point – a point that is consistently taught throughout the New Testament. One consequence of the transformation he effects in our lives is the way we now identify with his people. Yes, our justification before God is, indeed, by grace alone, received through personal faith alone. Salvation is the work of God alone, from beginning to end. But that justifying grace is no mere paper exercise, a heavenly pardon that makes no practical difference to the rest of our lives. It is applied to us by the Holy Spirit, who then dwells within us and continues to work in us. This is a spiritual reality that will be seen: in changed lives, changed perspectives, and changed motives. And one aspect of all this will be a new attitude to other Christians – because they are now our brothers and sisters in Christ. Yes, of course, Christians are to love all people – but the love we have for our fellow Christians is a very particular witness to, and *evidence of*, our faith in Christ. And evidence of faith is a key point in Jesus' parable, because it is a parable depicting final judgement.

We see an example of this transformation in the account of the Philippian jailer in Acts 16. Paul and Silas are in prison after their gospel witness to a demon-possessed slave girl so angers her owners that they have them arrested, beaten and charged. A sudden earthquake causes the prison doors to burst open and the prisoners' chains to be wrenched from the walls. The jailer's first concern is that the inmates will have used this opportunity to escape (which would have brought him personal disgrace and, quite possibly, execution). But when Paul and Silas reassure him, he is amazed. Although the account is condensed, they obviously share the gospel with him and he responds. But notice what happens next: "And he [the jailer] took them [Paul and Silas] the same hour of the night and washed their wounds... Then he brought them up into his house and set food before them. And he rejoiced, along with his entire household, that he had believed in God" (Acts 16:33,34).

Up to this point Paul and Silas were just two prisoners to be kept in custody; now they are his brothers in Christ! The care and compassion the jailer shows his (now) fellow Christians is evidence of his newfound faith in Jesus.

This is why the love Christians should have for one another is frequently referred to in the New Testament.

Paul sums up this principle for us in his letter to the Galatians: "So then, as we have opportunity, let us do good to everyone, and *especially to those who are of the household of faith*" (Galatians 6:10 – my italic).

The persevering faith of those young Christians in Thessalonica brought the Apostle Paul great joy – but, as we saw, it also encouraged him in the midst of his own afflictions.

And the same can be true for you and me today. The testimony of Christians in other parts of the world, who are maintaining a faithful witness in the face of opposition and hatred, can be a source of real joy and encouragement to us. Loving the body of Christ brings its blessing. Likewise, our engaging with the suffering of our fellow Christians, and loving them, in whatever way we are able, is a source of comfort and encouragement for them. Together we experience more of the reality of being part of the one church, the body of Christ.

Your response

1. Read 1 Thessalonians 2:13 - 3:5. How does the Apostle Paul respond to the possible impact of persecution on other Christians? What could you do today?

2. "If one member suffers, all suffer together," writes the Apostle Paul of the body of Christ (1 Corinthians 12:26). How should this principle affect our attitude to the persecution of other Christians?

3. We learn from persecution, not by pursuing a personal experience of it, but as the body of Christ. What might that mean for you and for the congregation you are part of?

Chapter 5

Focusing on the eternal

It has often been said that without 'hope' life quickly becomes miserable, and even intolerable. In short, we human beings need something to look forward to.

For some, this may mean the next exciting event on their social calendar: for others, hope may simply be about surviving and getting through another working week in order to enjoy the weekend. When we look further into the future, we might find ourselves hoping for good weather when we go on holiday; or that our children will get on in life; or that our football team wins the league next season (or avoids relegation...)

What do such hopes have in common? First, there is no certainty attached to them. In fact, depending on how narrowly you define the word 'hope', you might describe all of these examples as mere wishful thinking. If you have booked your holiday at a resort known for its sunshine, you have, perhaps, an increased chance of your hopes being realised; conversely, if you support a football team that has narrowly avoided relegation in the past three seasons, your hopes may be rather more precarious.

Secondly, from a Christian point of view, all of the hopes expressed above are *earthly*: they concern the things of this life. Many Christian hopes can also, in one sense, be about this life, too, at least initially. "I really hope my brother comes to the evangelistic supper on Saturday." "I really hope the new minister is someone who takes Bible teaching seriously." "I really hope my friend realises that what she is doing could lead her away from the Lord."

There is nothing inherently wrong with any of the expressions of hope we have cited (and the specifically Christian ones are, in fact, all very godly and laudable). Yet, none of them refers directly to *'the* hope' the New Testament talks about, the hope that, more than anything, should motivate our lives – the hope of eternal life in the glorious presence of God.

Keeping our eyes on *that* hope is not easy. Part of the problem is that this life is all we have really seen and experienced so far! We live in this world: a world of diaries, days, weeks and years; birth, marriage and death; health and sickness, happiness and sadness; work and rest, and then more work. But the problem is arguably made worse for Christians living in the West – because we have so much of *this* life to occupy our time and our thoughts. We've all heard that bit of homespun philosophy: "The more you have, the more you want." And, comparatively speaking, many of us in the West have an awful lot.

I have heard it said that, while Christians in the West are awestruck by what it must mean to live faithfully through persecution, their brothers and sisters in other parts of the world are equally amazed that one can remain faithful in the midst of worldliness and wealth. The reality is that both contexts are challenging and therefore both give opportunity to learn and to grow in faith and discipleship.

And so we come to the fifth and final way in which engaging with persecution can be a blessing to those of us seeking to follow Christ in the West. As we discover, meet and stand alongside those suffering for their Lord in circumstances we may find hard to envisage, their lives – and their faith – challenge a worldly view of hope, and help us to fix our eyes on the eternal.

Persecution magnifies hope

"For I consider that the sufferings of this present time are not worth comparing with the glory that is to be revealed to us," writes Paul in his letter to the Romans (Romans 8:18). At the beginning of this book, we suggested that in writing this Paul is probably thinking, first and foremost, of the kind of suffering we have been considering: suffering that comes our way *because* we are Christians. This is suggested by the previous verse in which Paul writes that Christians are "heirs of God and fellow heirs with Christ, provided we suffer with him in order that we may also be glorified with him" (Romans 8:17).

To "suffer with Christ" does not mean that we somehow share with him the burden of atoning for the sins of the world. Such a thought is totally alien to New Testament teaching about salvation. The Lord God laid his people's iniquities on Christ alone – and that work is finished and complete. Rather, the idea is bound up with our 'union with Christ', a key concept in the Apostle Paul's thinking and theology. By faith, we are spiritually united to Christ; that includes being united to him in his death and resurrection, for we experience the benefits of *his* death and resurrection. "For you have died, and your life is hidden with Christ in God. When Christ who is your life appears, then you also will appear with him in glory," Paul assures the Colossian Christians (Colossians 3:3,4). Notice the perspective (and tenses) there: in one sense, the Christian has *already* died.

Paul sometimes develops this theme to counter a

common criticism of the evangelical gospel. That criticism runs along these lines: if we are saved by faith alone, doesn't that mean we can live exactly how we want to and sin as much as we want to, so long as we 'believe'? No, says Paul, because to be justified by grace alone, through faith alone, is to be spiritually *united* to Jesus Christ, who is now our Lord. Even though, regrettably, Christians will, and do, sin, the fact is that in the depth of their renewed spiritual being they no longer want to: this inevitably means there is now a battle going on in their lives, between their sinful nature and their renewed life, that didn't exist prior to coming to faith (see Romans 6-7 and Galatians 2:15-21 for examples of this line of argument). So when Christians *do* sin, it should produce in them a godly grief that leads to repentance (see also 2 Corinthians 7:8-10).

On other occasions, Paul uses this concept of union with Christ in reference to our suffering for Jesus, which he can describe as a suffering *with* Christ, or a sharing of Christ's sufferings (eg 2 Corinthians 1:5; Philippians 3:10). An appreciation of this helps us understand one New Testament verse that many Christians find puzzling. In his letter to the Colossians, Paul writes: "Now I rejoice in my sufferings for your sake, and in my flesh I am filling up what is lacking in Christ's afflictions for the sake of his body, that is, the church" (Colossians 1:24).

On one level, the general sense of the verse is clear. Paul is reflecting on the fact that his suffering has been for the cause of the gospel and is proving to be for the benefit of the church. It is clear that Paul does not have in mind the common suffering of living in a fallen world; he is talking of *Christian* suffering for the gospel of Christ, and he can rejoice because he can see good coming from it. The difficulty lay in the phrase "what is lacking in

Christ's afflictions". We should not assume for one moment that Paul felt that Christ's *atoning sacrifice* was in any way defective, or needed adding to. But Christ suffered the opposition of a world in rebellion against God. So do his people – as Jesus himself promised they would (John 15:18-21). Our experience of that opposition is in spiritual union with Christ, and it is in that sense that we – in suffering for the gospel – are filling up what will be the total 'quota' (if we can use that word) of this suffering, a suffering of Christ's body that will continue until Christ returns in glory and triumph.

In Romans 8, then, Paul declares that our suffering with Christ – the persecution and suffering Christians experience because of their faith in, and union with, Christ – is "not worth comparing with the glory that is to be revealed to us" (Romans 8:18).

This in no way belittles or trivialises the suffering Christ's followers experience for their faith. Those of us who follow news bulletins from mission agencies, or have had the privilege of visiting parts of the world where Christians suffer for their faith, will no doubt have been deeply moved by what we hear.

I met a pastor from Plateau State in central Nigeria, whose wife, all six of his children and more than 60 members of his congregation were slaughtered in an attack by Islamic militants. I have met an Indian pastor whose teenage son was stabbed to death and whose daughter was abducted by Hindu fundamentalists – never to be seen again. Both attacks had been provoked by the pastors' gospel ministry. It would be monstrous to make light of stories such as this or to ignore the extent of human suffering experienced.

But the present suffering of Christ's church points us to the hope we have. Persecution for Christ and the gospel brings the hope inspired by that gospel into sharper focus, for our present comfort and consolation.

"If God is for us, who can be against us?" writes Paul later in the same chapter (Romans 8:31). If our perspective (not to mention our hope) were focused only on this life, we might be sorely tempted to answer: "Well, quite a lot can be against us, it seems!" On the other hand, if Paul's question implies the answer 'nothing' or 'no one' (which it does), it only makes sense in the light of eternity. Tribulation, distress and persecution – real though they undoubtedly are as present, painful experiences – do not separate us from the eternal love of Christ (Romans 8:35). It is in remembering this truth that persecution magnifies hope, for it brings the promise of eternity with Christ into sharp focus.

This, surely, is Paul's point in Romans 8:18. Far from dismissing the suffering of those who are persecuted for the gospel, Paul seeks to encourage them, and us, by lifting our spiritual eyes above the things of this life to focus on the sure and certain hope we have of experiencing and enjoying our full redemption in the glory-filled age to come.

Those who are living in the crucible of severe persecution around the world need this same pastoral care today. They need encouraging, and reminding of this eternal perspective and hope. As individuals and as churches we can contribute to that pastoral care by engaging with ministries that work alongside those who have suffered, and are suffering, for Christ and the gospel.

But, at the same time, do we Christians in the West not need reminding of this perspective ourselves? When we dwell too much on the things of this life and pursue as our priority the blessings of this life, are we not being squeezed into the world's mould? When the pervasive impact of worldliness dulls our awareness of God's kingdom, do we not need our spiritual gaze lifting upwards?

As we noted earlier, there are some Christians who do not want to be made to think about the persecution being experienced by brothers and sisters around the world – and they admit as much. But it is to our blessing to do so if we engage with the issue biblically, because then the lessons of this chapter and of the previous ones are brought before us. Then we are reminded that our true hope is not for this life, but for the life of the age to come. And this hope will definitely not disappoint us.

Hope makes sense of persecution

It is equally valuable to turn the issue on its head. If the reality and pain of persecution magnify and bring into focus our eternal hope, it is also true to say that understanding and meditating on our eternal hope make sense of the present experience of persecution.

In the New Testament, it is the resurrection of our Lord Jesus Christ that transforms our perspective on life. God, in his mercy, has "caused us to be born again to a living hope through the resurrection of Jesus Christ from the dead", declares the Apostle Peter (1 Peter 1:3). As the Apostle Paul puts it in his great chapter on resurrection: "If Christ has not been raised, your faith is futile and you are still in your sins. Then those also who have fallen asleep in Christ have perished. If in Christ we have hope in this life only, we are of all people most to be pitied" (1 Corinthians 15:17-19). If Christ has not been raised and has not given us a perspective that looks beyond this life into the age of eternity, then we might as well "eat and drink, for tomorrow we die", as Paul goes on to say

(1 Corinthians 15:32). But because Christ *has* been raised, and because we do therefore have a perspective that looks beyond the things of this life, Paul can conclude the chapter by declaring, "Therefore, my beloved brothers, be steadfast, immovable, always abounding in the work of the Lord, knowing that in the Lord your labour is not in vain" (1 Corinthians 15:58).

That last phrase is quite an assurance, if you pause to think about it. With the short-sighted view of this life only, we might be tempted to think that it *has* been in vain, at times, to engage in a particular gospel work. On a personal level, perhaps our prayerful determination to share the gospel with a neighbour has resulted in nothing but total apathy. Perhaps a parish mission has yielded little or no fruit – despite much prayer, planning and hard work. Looking further afield, perhaps we have heard of an evangelist or a pastor being martyred, church property burned down (and then, worse still, burned down a second time after being rebuilt), or Bibles and other Christian resources (made available by the giving of Christians from the more affluent West) confiscated or destroyed by those hostile to the gospel. In the short term, it is so easy to be discouraged at times, and to make the assessment that much prayerful work has been a waste of time and effort. But the New Testament hope, engendered by the resurrection of Christ, teaches us to see things through different eyes.

"And we know that for those who love God all things work together for good" (Romans 8:28), writes the Apostle Paul. This is a verse many Christians rightly cherish by faith. There may have been times in life when we have clung to its promise by our fingertips, as life's traumas have battered us. Yet, if in keeping with what we have previously suggested about Romans 8, Paul's thought here is primarily concerned with the outcome of suffering for Christ, we may not even know what that "good" is – at least not in this life. Hindsight is a wonderful thing, as we say. For some of Christ's saints, that hindsight won't come until they enter into their eternal inheritance.

Jesus Christ was willing to suffer to bring salvation for mankind. But we know he didn't stay dead. His death has a unique meaning – a meaning that was proven and proclaimed to the world in his resurrection. In following him, Christ calls his people to take up a cross for him, and to be willing to suffer for him. And the meaning, the value and the vindication of that suffering are only seen in the light of the final victory that is ours in Christ. The hope of that final victory makes sense of the persecution Christ's people presently suffer for him and the gospel.

More than once in this book, we have had occasion to refer to 2 Corinthians, and all that it teaches us about living with weakness. In chapter 4 of that letter, Paul, having just referred to the Christian's present afflictions and experience of persecution for the gospel, reminds his readers "that he who raised the Lord Jesus will raise us also with Jesus and bring us with you into his presence" (2 Corinthians 4:14). This hope is what motivates Paul to continue speaking the gospel, in the face of opposition and hostility. In the previous verse, he identifies himself with the writer of Psalm 116, who evidenced a faith that enabled him to speak out, even when greatly afflicted (see Psalm 116:10 which Paul quotes in 2 Corinthians 4:13). It is in the light of this that Paul can add: "So we do not lose heart. Though our outer self is wasting away, our inner self is being renewed day by day. For this light momentary affliction is preparing for us an eternal weight of glory beyond all comparison" (2 Corinthians 4:16,17).

"Affliction" is a word Paul uses on several occasions in 2 Corinthians, and it is worth emphasising again that he uses it to describe the experience of the minister of God's word, when the world expresses its opposition to that gospel.

If you are ever able to look down on a garden maze, perhaps from an upstairs window, you have a perspective on all the twists, turns and blind alleys that those who are down there, experiencing it, walking it and trying to find their way through it, don't have. In one sense we can't go and gaze down upon this life from eternity – but we can allow God's revelation in Scripture to equip us with something of that perspective. Meditating on the eternal hope we have can make sense of the persecution Christians presently suffer.

We see an illustration of this principle in Psalm 73, although the issue on this occasion is not persecution, but the apparent prosperity and ease of life enjoyed by the wicked.

Asaph the psalmist tells us how he felt when he observed this world through merely human eyes. "I was envious of the arrogant when I saw the prosperity of the wicked," he writes (Psalm 73:3). This perspective continues through the first half of the psalm. But then the turning point comes in verses 16 and 17. "But when I thought how to understand this, it seemed to me a wearisome task, until I went into the sanctuary of God; then I discerned their end." Under the old covenant, the sanctuary represented the presence of God, and the place of reconciliation with him. We might say he turns to God and to where God has revealed himself and reconciled us to himself. For us this now means coming to Jesus Christ as he is presented to us in the Scriptures. The second half of the psalm is then a testimony to renewed faith. In one sense the immediate circumstances may not have changed, and those he was tempted to gaze upon with envy were, in all probability, continuing to live it up. But with the eyes of faith he now saw the bigger picture. Notice the difference: "Whom have I in heaven but you? And there is nothing on earth that I desire besides you. My flesh and my heart may fail, but God is the strength of my heart and my portion forever. For behold, those who are far from you shall perish; you put an end to everyone who is unfaithful to you" (Psalm 73:25-27).

Meditating on the Bible's big themes – on Christ's work on the cross, on the resurrection hope, on God's great plan and purpose, on his righteousness, judgement and salvation – can help make sense of the present pain and suffering Christ's people may endure in a world that continues to reject him.

Persecution, hope and joy

In 'hope', we look to the future (even if that future is only a day away). 'Joy', on the other hand, is an emotion experienced in the present. And yet, for the Christian, the two are inextricably bound up. While the things of this life can certainly bring us considerable measures of joy, happiness, laughter, a sense of satisfaction and even personal fulfilment, we are ultimately those whose goal and purpose lie beyond this life.

Ironically, *Christian* joy is often seen most graphically and powerfully in the lives of those for whom this life brings little in the way of satisfaction, success or fulfilment – at least in the way those terms would be understood by the world around us. We read the biography of a Christian missionary who gave up a promising career to work in slums on the other side of the world. We witness the faith and palpable inner strength of a Christian who has suffered one disaster after another. And in the lives of Christ's persecuted people we will often see that Christian joy, writ large and in glorious Technicolor.

On a visit to Nigeria I attended a memorial service at a church where, a year earlier, an Islamist suicide bomber had wreaked devastation. Although the occasion no doubt brought back painful memories for all those present, there was an unmistakable sense of Christian joy in the singing and addresses given from the platform. This was a joy that is rooted in the unshakeable hope that each Christian has in and through the gospel.

On another occasion I met a group of Iranian Christians, who were taking part in a leadership training conference being held in another country. In my time with them several spoke of the stifling oppression they lived under in their homeland, with the threat of arrest constantly hanging over them – and yet there was a real exuberance and deep, spiritual joy among them.

Throughout this book, we have been arguing that the church in the West is blessed when it engages with issues of persecution, for it is a central New Testament theme and one that serves to refine and develop our discipleship. The joy that we witness among Christ's persecuted people is established, and sustained, not by their own resources and willpower, but by the grace of God. And yet both those living in the midst of severe persecution and we who are concerned for them need to learn to respond biblically. The body of Christ today needs to be taught, as the New Testament church was taught.

The letter that particularly encapsulates this teaching – and how hope and joy relate to persecution – is the first letter of the Apostle Peter.

Peter writes to church congregations in Asia who, in all probability, were facing sporadic, local harassment and opposition, rather than official state suppression (although that would eventually come). Their new life in Christ had put them at serious odds with pagan friends around them (1 Peter 4:4); slander and insult were becoming common experiences (1 Peter 3:16; 4:14). Peter writes to encourage them as they live under this cloud of persecution. And he encourages them by teaching them.

Throughout his letter, the perspective on life that lies behind everything Peter writes is that of suffering now, glory to come. This was, of course, the path that Christ willingly took. First-century Jewish Messianic expectation revolved around victory and glory. In particular, this was understood to involve the immediate, physical vanquishing of Israel's enemies by the Messiah. Jesus repudiated this popular notion of the Messiah and taught that – Messiah though he was – he had come to be rejected and killed. And yet there would indeed be glory for the Messiah one day, when his saving work on our behalf is fully revealed.

As we noted back in Chapter 1 of this book, Peter, at the very moment of acknowledging that Jesus was the Messiah, refused to accept this agenda (Mark 8:27-38). By the time he writes his first letter, Peter is a changed man. Not only has he witnessed the crucifixion (and resurrection) of his Lord, he has also lived through the failure and shame of renouncing his Lord in the face of personal danger. But Peter has experienced the forgiveness and restoration of the risen Lord Jesus. Furthermore, he is the first Apostle fearlessly to proclaim that the suffering and death of Jesus are central to God's plan and purpose for the salvation of mankind (Acts 2).

Peter addresses his readers as "elect exiles" (1 Peter

1:1). In all probability this was not because they were, literally, exiles, but because the phrase sums up the paradox of being a Christian: chosen by God (and so secure), and yet at the same time passing through a world that is not our real home. We who cling to the stuff of this life too tightly need to allow this description to mould first our thinking and then our behaviour.

'Hope' is the first major theme of the letter (1 Peter 1:3-21). (Notice how references to hope bracket this section in verses 3 and 21.) For every Christian has been "born again to a living hope through the resurrection of Jesus Christ from the dead" (1 Peter 1:3). As such we have a heavenly inheritance that cannot be taken away from us (1 Peter 1:4). Notably, Peter then declares: "In this you rejoice, though now for a little while, if necessary, you have been grieved by various trials" (1 Peter 1:6). These trials (opposition for being a Christian is probably what Peter is primarily referring to) can serve to test the genuineness of our faith.

At the end of the letter, Peter sums up his purpose in writing: "I have written briefly to you, exhorting and declaring that this is the true grace of God. Stand firm in it" (1 Peter 5:12). Christians live in a hostile world, for it is a world that stands opposed to the Lord Jesus Christ and to God's kingdom. We have been reminded of that already, during the course of this book. God's grace is needed in such an environment if we are to live lives that are a faithful testimony to Christ – and this is particularly so when we are exposed to the world's hatred and insult. When we endure in the face of such opposition, we are following in the footsteps of Jesus himself. "He committed no sin, neither was deceit found in his mouth. When he was reviled, he did not revile in return; when he suffered, he did not threaten, but continued entrusting himself to him who judges justly" (1 Peter 2:22,23).

It is to help them to live faithfully in this hostile world that Peter writes. Christians are to remember the nature of their hope and live holy lives as a consequence (1 Peter 1:3-21); they are to remember that they are now numbered among God's people, whom they are to love "earnestly" (1 Peter 1:22 – 2:10); they are to behave honourably and respectfully in the various spheres of life in which they find themselves (1 Peter 2:11 – 3:12); they are to be ready to explain the hope they have – even if this brings suffering (1 Peter 3:13 - 4:6); and they are to go on serving each other to the glory of God (1 Peter 4:7-11).

And yet, despite the repeated references to the opposition of the world, this is no mere grin-and-bear-it mentality that Peter urges upon them.

"Beloved, do not be surprised at the fiery trial when it comes upon you to test you, as though something strange were happening to you. But rejoice insofar as you share Christ's sufferings, that you may also rejoice and be glad when his glory is revealed. If you are insulted for the name of Christ, you are blessed, because the Spirit of glory and of God rests upon you" (1 Peter 4:12-14).

These three verses take us to the heart, I believe, of Peter's understanding of a Christian life lived in the midst of a hostile world. They show us how Peter saw persecution, hope and joy bound up together. They are verses that are deeply challenging to anything that smacks of superficial Christian faith. They are verses we Christians in the West would do well to reflect on at length.

First, Christians are not to be surprised when persecution occurs (1 Peter 4:12). Sadly, however, we often are. In Chapter 2, we looked at the spiritual reasons that lay behind the persecution of Christ's followers, and so we don't need to dwell on them again here, except to reiterate the point that if we understand human nature biblically, and understand the gospel biblically, we won't be surprised when persecution occurs. Jesus' teaching at the Last Supper clearly lies behind Peter's words, and he wants his readers to hold on to that biblical worldview. By the same token we Christians in the West desperately need to be cultivating congregations of believers whose worldview and understanding of humanity are shaped by the Scriptures – not by the prevailing wisdom of the world around us.

However, Peter's readers are to maintain that worldview not merely in a spirit of grim resignation. The Apostle is far more positive – and pastoral – than that. He describes the experience of severe persecution as a "fiery trial" that "tests". Some modern translations that omit the word "fiery" unfortunately obscure the imagery behind Peter's words, which is that of the process of refining precious metals.

The word translated "test" can have either a negative or a positive connotation. The journalist who 'tests' a senior politician with a series of tricky questions is probably looking to trip him up. The sports player who 'tests' his opponent's game is certainly looking for a weakness to exploit. But Peter is using the concept of 'testing' in a more positive sense, with the goodness and grace of a loving and sovereign God in view. This is the 'testing' that is intended to produce something purer, the testing that refines.

As we saw, Peter has already used this testing, or refining, imagery earlier in the letter. In the opening chapter, having reminded them of their heavenly inheritance, he writes: "In this you rejoice, though now for a little while, if necessary, you have been grieved by various trials, so that the tested genuineness of your faith – more precious than gold that perishes though it is tested by fire – may be found to result in praise and glory and honour at the revelation of Jesus Christ" (1 Peter 1:6,7).

Gold is put through a 'refiner's fire' in order to burn off the impurities and to produce something of greater purity. Peter's point (both in 1 Peter 1 and in 1 Peter 4:12) is that God can use the suffering of his people to produce in them a stronger faith. (When he refers in 1 Peter 1:7 to gold "perishing", it is probably to contrast the fact that gold – even when purified – ultimately belongs to this world, and so will one day perish; faith, by contrast, bears fruit in the eternal age to come.)

This does not mean that the experience of persecution is simply water off a duck's back to the Christian: as we said earlier in this chapter, we have no right to belittle the intense reality of suffering for Christ that others have, or are experiencing. But, at the same time, there is real encouragement in being reminded that God's good purposes transcend any present suffering.

Secondly, Christians are to rejoice that persecution confirms our eternal hope (1 Peter 4:13). When Christians suffer simply because they are Christians, it shows they belong to Christ because they are participating in the sufferings of Christ himself. We noted earlier that this does not mean we contribute to his atoning work but that, in our spiritual union with him, we share with him in suffering at the hands of those who are opposed to God and his kingdom.

The 'rejoicing' Peter speaks of in this verse is *not* a rejoicing in the suffering itself. This is not about being a hero, like the star of a Hollywood action movie, who takes a few bullets from the baddies but bravely, doggedly, fights his way through the enemy lines to rescue his best buddy. Nor is it that attitude of self-pity, which draws attention to self by making sure everyone knows 'how hard life has been'.

"But rejoice insofar as you share Christ's sufferings, that you may also rejoice and be glad when his glory is revealed" (1 Peter 4:13). Do you see where Peter puts his emphasis? It is not in the suffering in and of itself, but in the knowledge (albeit highlighted and illustrated by that suffering) that we are united to Christ. The experience of being persecuted because of our faith in Christ confirms that we belong to him. And this knowledge in turn serves as an assurance for the future, "that you may also rejoice and be glad when his glory is revealed". Although Peter doesn't spell it out explicitly, the strong implication at the end of the verse is 'because you share Christ's sufferings now, you will *also share* Christ's glory when it is revealed'. In other words, if persecution serves to remind us of our union with Christ, it also reminds us of our heavenly hope.

Thirdly, in the midst of the experience of persecution, Christians know the blessing of God's presence *now*. As we have just noted, the overall thrust of 1 Peter 4:13 is toward the future, for we are being reminded that one day we will share in Christ's glory. In 1 Peter 4:14, however, Peter shifts to the present: "If you are insulted for the name of Christ, you are blessed because the Spirit of glory and of God rests upon you."

Given that the context is that of passing through a "fiery trial" of suffering for Christ, the promise of God's Spirit 'resting' on the believer (who, as a believer, is after all already indwelt by that Spirit) should naturally be taken to refer to the promise of strengthening in the hour of need.

The thought being expressed may be similar, if

perhaps broader, to that of Jesus, who told his disciples: "When they deliver you over, do not be anxious how you are to speak or what you are to say, for what you are to say will be given to you in that hour. For it is not you who speak, but the Spirit of your Father speaking through you" (Matthew 10:19,20). Peter is thinking not just of the Spirit giving us the right words in the hour of persecution – but of giving us the strength to endure.

And yet Peter also refers here to the 'Spirit of *glory* resting on us'. Under the old covenant, God's glory rested upon, and filled, the tabernacle, the place where God met with his people and was reconciled to them (Exodus 40:34,35). This function of the tabernacle was fulfilled in the person and work of Jesus, who reconciles man to God (as promised in Isaiah 11:2 and evidenced at Jesus' baptism: Matthew 3:16,17). Because Jesus is the fulfilment of all that the tabernacle/temple stood for, as the place where God dwells, this blessing in turn extends to Christ's followers: those who are united to him by faith. We, both individually and collectively, are therefore now the 'temple of the Spirit' (see, for example, 1 Corinthians 3:16; 1 Corinthians 6:19; Ephesians 2:19-22) because Jesus Christ is pre-eminently the temple of the Spirit. In the previous verse (1 Peter 4:13), as we have seen, Peter refers to the future manifestation of Christ's glory. The strengthening of God's Spirit – something we can know *now* in and through the opposition we face for Christ – becomes further confirmation that we are God's and will one day share in the eternal glory of Christ.

This is rich, biblical, pastoral encouragement that the church of Jesus Christ needs to hear and to dwell on. Those who are living – now – in the midst of the fieriest trials of persecution need to hear this. But so do we who presently experience greater freedom in our faith, for what Peter would have us understand is fundamental to standing firm, by the grace of God, in a world that is hostile to the Lord and to the gospel.

Furthermore, if we in the West are prepared to engage deeply with the lives of those who are suffering for the gospel, we will discover the truth of these great promises being lived out today. In recent years, I have found it tremendously encouraging to read the testimonies of those Christians who have so obviously known that strengthening of God in the face of opposition. I remember the story of one Vietnamese evangelist who had endured several months in solitary confinement and regular beatings and who, as the full weight of that country's legal system was bearing down on him, continued to praise God for opportunities that a lengthy prison sentence would give him to share the gospel with others. His story reminded me again of Paul and Silas who, after being arrested in Philippi, and accused of disturbing the peace - and after being beaten and imprisoned - sat chained in their prison cell praying and singing hymns to God (Acts 16:20-25)! This is thanks to the Spirit of God, resting on his persecuted people, strengthening and sustaining them.

Persecution, hope and the word of God

But, as we have just noted in our observations of 1 Peter, this strengthening comes as God's people are grounded in the teaching of God's word. Psalm 119 is a stirring example of a faith and a devotional life rooted in the truth of that word – and which is therefore equipped to face the world and its hostility. The psalm is well known for being the longest – at 176 verses. It is also a wonderfully crafted piece of writing. The writer has divided the psalm into 22 sections (one for each letter of the Hebrew alphabet) of eight lines each. He has then shaped a poetic acrostic, with the eight lines in each section beginning with the appropriate Hebrew letter (although this feature is lost in the translation into English).

This attention to the Hebrew alphabet is apt, given that the psalm is, first and foremost, an extended meditation on God's word, and on the joy of believing it, trusting it and adhering to it.

But although this is the psalm's main theme, an interesting sub-plot that runs through it is the opposition that the psalmist is evidently facing for his faith and particularly for his allegiance to God's truth. Yet, in and through all of this, it is that same word of truth that sustains him. "Even though princes sit plotting against me, your servant will meditate on your statutes. Your testimonies are my delight; they are my counsellors," he declares (Psalm 119:23,24). Later he writes: "This is my comfort in my affliction, that your promise gives me life" (Psalm 119:50). What a wonderful summary that is of a life lived by the grace of God and established by the word of God.

The psalmist knows that those who afflict him stand opposed to the purposes of God. "They draw near who persecute me with evil purpose; they are far from your law. But you are near, O Lord, and all your commandments are true" (Psalm 119:150,151). Again: "Look on my affliction and deliver me, for I do not forget your law. Plead my cause and redeem me; give me life according to your promise! Salvation is far from the wicked, for they do not seek your statutes" (Psalm 119:153-155). As we saw back in Chapter 2, when the world hates Christians, it is demonstrating its rejection of Christ and its ignorance of God.

On several occasions, we see the psalmist leaning on God's word in the face of that opposition. "Princes persecute me without cause, but my heart stands in awe of your words. I rejoice at your word like one who finds great spoil" (Psalm 119:161,162), he declares. This truly biblical faith sustains his hope in the salvation that comes from the Lord.

Persecution from a world that is hostile to the gospel can, under the sovereign hand of God, sharpen our focus on the eternal nature of our Christian hope. The reality of suffering in this life for the gospel throws into sharper relief the fact that, ultimately, our hope in Christ is not for this life, but for the life of the age to come. At the same time, the more we allow God's word to set our agenda and shape our perspective, the better equipped we will be to come to terms with the reality and the experience of opposition and persecution for the sake of Christ in this life.

This will be true for those presently living in the midst of oppression and violence for their faith. But it is also true for those of us who have greater freedom to worship and serve the Lord Jesus. And so to commit ourselves to care, to get involved in the encouraging, the supporting, the equipping and the praying for our persecuted brothers and sisters, is to have our own spiritual eyes lifted to gaze upon the sure and certain hope we have in Christ Jesus our Lord.

To do so is, indeed, to be blessed. To do so is to be better equipped to do good for God.

Your response

1. Read 1 Peter 4:12-14. How, according to Peter, are blessing, joy and hope to be found in the midst of persecution?
2. To what extent is your life shaped by, and driven by, the eternal hope we have as Christians?
3. Persecution for Christ and the gospel brings the hope inspired by that gospel into sharper focus. To what extent is that statement true?

Conclusion

The end of the beginning?

Persecution is, indeed, a challenging topic. As one particular facet of suffering, it challenges our faith in a sovereign, loving God. It challenges the comfort – or the comparative comfort – that many of us are used to in the West. It certainly challenges us to reflect on the reality and extent of our own commitment to Jesus Christ. It reminds us that in this life we remain jars of clay: ordinary vessels of God's powerful gospel.

This can be an uncomfortable experience. Persecution is not something we want to experience personally and, as Christians in the so-called 'free' West, it has probably not featured prominently in our own walk with the Lord, however long we have been his followers. It is tempting, therefore, to park it among the vast array of Christian mission activities that we may, from time to time, take an interest in. Of course, if pressed, we would say we are concerned for Christian brothers and sisters who suffer for their faith in other parts of the world (and how could we not be?) But, then again, there are so many needs in our world, aren't there?

However, persecution is not simply one subject among many that we might take a compassionate interest in. Through the course of this book, we have been suggesting something different.

Once you have eyes to see it, it is evident that

persecution – suffering for Christ; suffering that might otherwise be avoided if you did not maintain a visible allegiance to Christ - is everywhere in the New Testament. Jesus warned his disciples of it, and the apostolic writers of the epistles both experienced it and wrote of it as a fundamental aspect of Christian discipleship. Persecution can be a danger to faith, make no mistake; but equally – by the grace of God – it can be something that leads to the refining and the deepening of faith.

New Testament teaching that addresses the theme of persecution and suffering is meant to be heard by the whole church. We hear it not by diluting the primary meaning of the biblical texts or rushing to broaden the scope of its application, but by remembering that we are part of the one body of Christ. "You *are* the persecuted church!" a colleague of mine said to a gathering of Western Christians who had come to hear about what is happening around the world. And that is the perspective we need to have: there is one body of Christ, and it experiences persecution from a world that rejects Christ and the gospel. Severe persecution (in whatever form that may take) may not be *our* personal experience in this part of the world, at this moment in history, but we should identify with those people – those parts of the body – for whom that *is* presently an all too common experience. Persecution is never uniform, in geography, intensity or severity. But the body of Christ *will* be persecuted.

So what are we meant to hear? What are we meant to understand?

We have suggested that persecution helps us to learn important lessons of discipleship in five key areas of the Christian life: mission, the gospel, grace, the church and hope.

Engaging with persecution challenges errors or distortions we in the West are prone to in these five key areas.

It challenges a simplistic and triumphalist view of mission and the part we are to play in that mission. It reminds us of that key principle: that God's grace works through human weakness. Mission is not about us impressing the world; it is about God, working through us – even when the world despises us.

It challenges a consumerist view of the message we proclaim, by sharpening our understanding of the gospel and by showing why the gospel is God's answer to man's deepest need. We have no mandate to mould or to adorn our message in order to make it more appealing to others. Persecution reminds us that it is the *natural* response of mankind to reject the gospel – the gospel we are to go on proclaiming. Only by God's grace do any of us accept that gospel.

It challenges a self-sufficient view of life – in which many become so accustomed to coping and succeeding in their own strength – by deepening our desire for that grace of God. The sovereign grace that is needed to come to faith is the grace that is needed to continue in the faith. Nowhere is this more obvious than in situations where suffering comes because of that faith.

It challenges an overly individualistic view of the Christian life by broadening our understanding and experience of what it truly means to be part of the body of Christ. Individual, personal faith is lived out through the witness of that body. So when parts of the body are suffering, we are to share in that suffering.

And it challenges a worldly view of hope by keeping our spiritual eyes fixed on the eternal things of the age to come, for it is the eternal aspect of hope that helps make sense of the transitory sufferings of this life.

None of this, however, means that we should yearn for severe persecution to come upon us in the West. Rather, these principles should motivate us to engage more closely with those Christians who are living in the crucible of real suffering for Christ. As we do this, we can learn from them – but also with them – the biblical perspective and lessons we have outlined in this book.

At times that may mean we need to resource our severely persecuted brothers and sisters, particularly in contexts where they have been starved of strong pastoral leadership and good biblical teaching. At the risk of sounding patronising or overly paternal, our grasp of the theological reasons for the persecution they have been experiencing may actually, in some situations, be stronger than theirs. At other times, however, we may simply need to listen to the testimonies our persecuted brothers and sisters are giving – and rejoice before our God for the tangible, flesh-and-blood reminders they give us of the ever-sufficient, all-sustaining grace of God.

I have rather enigmatically sub-titled this concluding chapter "The end of the beginning?" The major themes and the underlying premise of this book have been strongly suggestive of the importance and the value of real, meaningful, active engagement with persecution and the lives of those members of the body of Christ who are enduring severe persecution. We have talked about 'engaging meaningfully' with our persecuted brothers and sisters, but what does this mean in practical terms and, crucially, how do we begin to do so? As we conclude, it may help to bear in mind two overarching and fundamental responses we can make to the persecution of our fellow Christians.

Prayer commitment

Prayer is one of those things that we are often better at talking about than actually doing. It is good to hear sermons about prayer and to read books on prayer – provided that as a result of our learning we actually *do* some praying!

At the same time, prayer is one of those things we can easily be made to feel guilty about. Perhaps we don't pray enough. Perhaps when we do pray we have begun to realise how selfish our prayers are. In one sense, of course, we pray for the things that concern us – and for things we are familiar with. I am all too well aware of my own frailties, weaknesses and sins: there is no shortage of prayer material in my own selfish, sinful heart! At the same time, I know about (and care about) things that concern my family and friends, my church family and work colleagues.

But intercessory prayer that moves beyond our immediate circle of acquaintance and knowledge requires us to be *informed*. We need to know what (and who) we are praying about, and why.

The first reported case of persecution after the ascension of Jesus comes in Acts 4, with the arrest of Peter and John. This had followed the incident at the Jerusalem temple when a man was healed (Acts 3:1-10). Peter had taken the opportunity to preach the gospel, calling on people to repent (Acts 3:11-26). The two apostles were arrested by the temple police and brought before the Jewish council, where Peter had boldly testified further to the resurrection of Jesus (Acts 4:5-12). This was the very thing (rather than the healing) that had so annoyed the Jewish authorities in the first place (Acts 4:2)! Not surprisingly, the upshot was that the council, having questioned them, threatened them and demanded that they stop speaking and teaching in the name of Jesus.

What happens next is very instructive. "When they were released, they went to their friends and *reported* what the chief priests and the elders had said to them" (Acts 4:23). The disciples' first instinct is to pray: "And when they heard it, they lifted their voices together to God..." (Acts 4:24). Somebody once said that, for the Christian, prayer is not the last resort; it is the *first* resort – or, at least, should be. But prayer needs to be *informed*. We are not told if the disciples had already been praying (though we might assume they were aware of the arrest of Peter and John). Even if they had been, their prayers are now further shaped by the report Peter and John had brought back. The two apostles had been threatened and told to stop preaching about Jesus – and it is this news that prompts the disciples to pray very specifically: "Lord, look upon their threats and grant to your servants to continue to speak your word with all boldness" (Acts 4:29). And of course their prayer is gloriously answered! In the short term, Luke tells us: "They were all filled with the Holy Spirit and continued to speak the word of God with boldness" (Acts 4:31). In the longer term, the rest of the Book of Acts testifies to their continued boldness in preaching the gospel.

Although, in this instance, those who prayed were close friends of Peter and John, we can, I hope, appreciate the point: if we are to intercede for persecuted brothers and sisters today, we need to be informed. If our prayers are to move beyond the bland and general, if we are going to pray specifically for real people with real needs, we need to acquire the information, and we need to do so regularly. It is as simple as that.

It also helps to understand something of the context in which Christians are suffering persecution for their faith –

not least because we need to pray for their persecutors as well as the persecuted (see Jesus' command in Matthew 5:44). This, too, will require that we are being informed.

In giving instructions for church life and worship, Paul wrote to Timothy: "First of all, then, I urge that supplications, prayers, intercessions, and thanksgivings be made for all people, for kings and for all who are in high positions, that we may lead a peaceful and quiet life, godly and dignified in every way" (1 Timothy 2:1,2).

It has often been pointed out what a remarkable statement this is, given that at the time Paul wrote to Timothy, the Emperor of the Roman Empire was the notorious Nero, hardly the most benign or just ruler the world has ever known! But Paul is adamant that the church should pray for those in authority. Why? As ever, Paul has God's kingdom and the ministry of the gospel at the forefront of his mind. Peaceful conditions (which must include freedom of conscience and freedom of religion) enable the propagation and spread of the gospel. As Paul goes on: "This is good, and it is pleasing in the sight of God our Saviour, who desires all people to be saved and to come to the knowledge of the truth" (1 Timothy 2:3,4).

A commitment to pray for our persecuted brothers and sisters will require us to be informed regularly of what is happening where and what issues and people we should be bringing before the Lord.

Practical compassion

The second basic response to the persecution of our fellow Christians around the world should be practical compassion. Earlier in the book we were reminded of the exhortation in the letter to the Hebrews: "Remember those who are in prison, as though in prison with them, and those who are mistreated, since you also are in the body" (Hebrews 13:3).

But what does it mean, in this instance, to 'remember'? The whole paragraph – introduced by the phrase "Let brotherly love continue" (Hebrews 13:1) – is intensely practical. Sometimes 'remembering' may mean no more than our ability to recall facts and figures, but at other times 'remembering' means more than that: it is an act that will engage us and involve us. Think, for example, of *remembering* someone in our will, or *remembering* someone's birthday. Both go beyond the mere recollection of information and involve us in practical ways. Such is the meaning and intention of the writer's words in Hebrews 13:3.

The 'brotherly love' of which the writer to the Hebrews refers is a major theme in the first letter of John. John writes to counter some dangerous, insidious false teaching that threatened to undermine the true, Apostolic gospel and, in particular, a true understanding of the person and work of Jesus Christ. As he writes, John's thinking rotates around three key themes: doctrine, obedience and love. As we read 1 John, we find that he keeps coming back to these key themes, from different perspectives.

In chapter three John writes, "For this is the message that you have heard from the beginning, that we should love one another. We should not be like Cain, who was of the evil one and murdered his brother. And why did he murder him? Because his own deeds were evil and his brother's righteous" (1 John 3:11,12).

As we saw earlier, 'brotherly love' is an important testimony to the reality of Christian faith. John then cites the example of Cain's murder of his brother Abel. Cain was reacting to the way Abel had been accepted by the

Lord (see Genesis 4:1-5). In doing so, Cain typifies the spiritual condition of the 'world', which exists in opposition to the Lord. This is why, in the next verse, John adds the comment: "Do not be surprised, brothers, that the world hates you" (1 John 3:13). The hatred of Christians and of all they stand for reveals the world 'in its true colours', as we might say, for (as we saw back in Chapter 2) in persecuting the followers of Jesus Christ, the world's attitude to Christ himself is made evident.

Christians, clearly, should be different: "We know that we have passed out of death into life, because we love the brothers" (1 John 3:14). This (coupled, in 1 John 3:16, with the reminder that Christ's love for us was a practical love that led to his death in our place) leads John to a very practical application, as far as his readers are concerned. "If anyone has the world's goods and sees his brother in need, yet closes his heart against him, how does God's love abide in him? Little children, let us not love in word or talk but in deed and in truth" (1 John 3:17,18).

John's words earth in a very clear, practical way what we were considering in Chapter 4 regarding the love that ought to be seen within the body of Christ. Where parts of that body are suffering – because of the world's rejection of the Christ they stand for and preach – the other parts of the body should be prepared to step in, with hearts open towards them, to help provide for their needs, physical or spiritual.

As individual Christians and as local Christian communities, we clearly cannot support every good Christian work that is going on around the world. At times, the needs can seem overwhelming. If you've ever wandered past mission society stands at a Christian conference or event, you will know what I mean. It is helpful, however, to reflect from time to time on what we *are* currently engaged in and supporting. Is it balanced? In what way does it echo the priorities of the New Testament?

Surely we ought to be making *some* space in our mission thinking, praying and supportive activity for our persecuted brothers and sisters in Christ? The prevalence of persecution as a New Testament theme, the important consequences of seeing ourselves as part of the body of Christ, and the discipleship lessons and blessings that emanate from a willingness to suffer for Christ all point in that direction.

A commitment to pray that requires us to be informed. A practical compassion that requires us to act. Here are two fundamental ways to respond to the reality of persecution around the world today. To begin to respond in these ways will be to your blessing, and to the blessing of the body of Christ. As such, it will be to the glory of God.

We began this book with two quotes, one of which was from the Apostle Paul. It is appropriate to return to that quote as we close.

It reminds us Christians in the West why we should take suffering for Christ seriously; why we need to allow it to be part of our thinking, learning and praying.

Paul begins the fifth chapter of his letter to the Romans by declaring that, through the glorious gospel of our Lord Jesus Christ (when applied to us by the Spirit and received by faith), we have been justified before God. We have peace with God, and therefore access to God, and we rejoice in the hope of the glory of God. Hallelujah.

But then Paul adds: "More than that, we rejoice in our sufferings, knowing that suffering produces endurance, and endurance produces character, and character produces hope, and hope does not put us to shame, because God's love has been poured into our hearts through the Holy Spirit who has been given to us" (Romans 5:3-5).

May we, and all who suffer for the Lord Jesus Christ, know the truth of that in our lives, today and always.

Release International

Our vision is to see a world in which the whole Body of Christ understands persecution and responds prayerfully, pastorally and practically every time a Christian is persecuted.

You may like to read *Tortured For Christ,* which was written by Richard Wurmbrand, the Romanian pastor who inspired the founding of Release in 1968. Pastor Wurmbrand wrote this book after being imprisoned for a total of 14 years by the Romanian authorities in the 1950s and 1960s. The book is a classic story of Christian faith and endurance under extreme pressure. Throughout his time in prison Pastor Wurmbrand was tortured and brainwashed, yet he developed and maintained a Christ-like attitude of love and 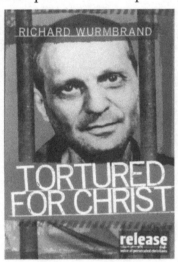 forgiveness towards his tormentors. The book is his inspiring story, his reflections on the persecution of Christians and his call to the Church in the West to remember its persecuted brothers and sisters around the world who even today are suffering for the sake of Jesus Christ.

Tortured For Christ is available from:
Release International
Tel: 01689 823491
Email: info@releaseinternational.org or visit:
www.releaseinternational.org